The Party

A Guide to Adventurous Entertaining

SALLY QUINN

Illustrations by Susan Davis

Simon & Schuster

SIMON & SCHUSTER
Rockefeller Center
1230 Avenue of the Americas
New York, NY 10020

SIMON & SCHUSTER and colophon are registered trademarks
of Simon & Schuster Inc.

Manufactured in the United States of America

1   3   5   7   9   10   8   6   4   2

Library of Congress Cataloging-in-Publication Data
Quinn, Sally.
The party : adventures in entertaining / Sally Quinn ;
illustrations by Susan Davis.
p.   cm.
1. Entertaining.
2. Washington (D.C.)—Social life and customs.   I. Title.
GV1471.Q55   1997
642'.4—dc21   97-29874
CIP
ISBN 0-684-81144-8

To my parents, Bette and Bill Quinn,

who taught me that successful entertaining is

really about generosity of spirit

Contents

"General Quinn,
in this house we do not smoke until after the sweet."

A while ago a producer on *Good Morning America* called me in Washington and asked me if I would come up to New York and be on the show. It was right before Christmas and they were doing a week of "Holiday Entertaining" segments. At first I refused. After all, I was a serious journalist and this was a totally frivolous subject. It would ruin my reputation. Jackie Leo was persuasive, however, and also, there was a party I wanted to go to in New York the night before, so I finally said yes.

When I arrived at the studio the morning of the show, Jackie told me that I would be introduced as a "society hostess." I nearly fainted. I implored her not to have me introduced as a hostess. Being called a "Washington hostess" was bad enough, though at least that had a political connotation. But "society hostess"? How had I managed to get myself into this, anyway? Was it too late to get out of it? Before I knew it I was whisked into Makeup, taken down to the greenroom, and summoned into the studio. I was seated at a dining room table that was set with china and silver and party napkins, across from my host, Charlie Gibson. It was getting worse by the minute.

"We have invited," he was saying to the camera, "author, journalist, and"—he looked at me, quizzically it seemed—"sometime Washington hostess, Sally Quinn . . ."

The dreaded word.

"The first time," I demurred, with less than total candor and with a slightly embarrassed laugh, "I've ever been described as a hostess. . . ."

Charlie looked betrayed. If I wasn't a hostess, what was I doing on the "Holiday Entertaining" segment?

We climbed over that hurdle and segued nicely into a discussion of party rules. I suggested that it was important to stay in-formed, to read the paper. I was behaving perfectly until Charlie asked me, "What happens if conversation lags? What do you do?"

"Well," I responded brightly, "as I said, I think, you watch the *Today Show* . . ." The words weren't out of my mouth before I realized what I had just said.

But Charlie was not about to let me get away with that. *"Good Morning America!"* he corrected in mock horror.

What could I do but fling my head down on the table and cover it with my hands?

Afterward I was greeted by chilly smiles and wan "well done's," and I escaped as quickly as possible.

But I did begin to think about the word "hostess" and what it means.

The dictionary defines "hostess" as "a female host; a woman who serves in the capacity of a host." A "host" is "a person who receives or entertains guests in his own home or elsewhere." There's certainly nothing offensive there.

"A person who receives or entertains guests in his own home" doesn't really sound like someone to be disdained, and generally the word "host" is not a derisive term. After all, who among us has not at least offered someone something to drink in his or her own home? I can hardly think of the person who could not at some point be described as a "host." The word "hostess," however, has come to mean (if not in the dictionary, at least in the vernacu-lar) a frivolous woman with nothing better to do than give parties.

And certainly nobody would ever have asked my husband then, or today, to go on *Good Morning America* to discuss holiday entertaining, even though he is a great host and likes to be in-volved in the planning of all our parties. Can anyone imagine ever referring to him as "host Ben Bradlee"?

Years ago, in the days of legendary Washington hostesses such as Perle Mesta and Gwen Cafritz, playing that role was one of the few ways women of intelligence and ambition could accrue power. Successful hostesses were revered. For these women, entertaining was their life. It was their job.

One of my first jobs in Washington after graduating from college was as social secretary to the Algerian ambassador, Cherif Guellal. It was 1967 when I went to work at the embassy. Washington party giving was in full swing, and the role of hostess was still an admired one. Certainly Cherif, who was a glamorous thirty-two-year-old bachelor, was one of the most celebrated hosts in the city.

Two years later, when I began covering parties for the *Washington Post* "Style" section, one could already sense the change in atmosphere. It was the late sixties, the Vietnam War was raging, feminism was on the rise, and all of our social values were being questioned in a fundamental way. In that context, parties and hostesses really did not seem appropriate.

Women began rejecting the role of hostess. They went out and joined social movements, got jobs, became activists. They took friends out to restaurants, or simply didn't entertain at all. It became almost a badge of honor to say, "I never entertain." The worst, the most dismissive, thing you could have said about another woman, in Washington, at least, was that she was "just a hostess."

"The Washington hostess" was rapidly becoming extinct.

By the early seventies writer Barbara Howar summed it up: "If I thought my epitaph would read HOSTESS I'd refuse to die."

She didn't die, but the Washington hostess did. And nobody mourned her. At first.

Somewhere along the line it became clear that something was missing. The truth was that we had lost one of the most important avenues of social communication and because of that, things just weren't as much fun anymore.

Ten years ago I would never have allowed myself to be persuaded to go on *Good Morning America* to discuss holiday entertaining. It would have been too humiliating. We were still all locked into the notion that women should be involved only in "serious" ventures.

And yet, and yet . . . entertaining today is a multibillion-dollar industry in this country, not to mention around the world. Women, and men too, in many professions must entertain as part of their careers. The idea that it was demeaning to "receive or entertain guests" in one's home seemed to lose credence.

The President and the First Lady (our country's First Host and Hostess) routinely entertain around forty thousand guests in the White House just in the few weeks before Christmas. And in the first four years of their administration, the Clintons spent over $3.5 million on parties. That's political entertaining.

One of the main roles of ambassadors is entertaining. That's diplomatic. Major corporations all over the world have huge expense accounts and entertainment allowances. That's commercial. And American taxpayers even subsidize individuals and companies by allowing tax deductions for entertaining business associates.

There is nothing frivolous, shallow, or irrelevant about entertaining when you're talking about that kind of money, energy, time, and commitment, which both men and women, professionally and privately, expend for mere parties.

And never mind the big money; think about your five-year-old's birthday party. What about the hamburgers and hot dogs, potato salad and baked beans you served at the Fourth of July barbecue or the tea party for your grandmother's ninetieth birthday? That's entertaining.

Imagine Bedouins in their tents serving lamb to a visitor, Eskimos producing fish for some explorers, an Amazonian tribe welcoming tourists with a special drink. That's it too.

We all do it. Everyone entertains someone sometimes. It's part of social life. So if you're going to do it, you might as well do it right.

How do you do it right?

Just follow the Golden Rule. "Do unto others . . ." Treat your guests the way you would like to be treated. It's as simple as that.

I like to go to parties. I like to give them. Over the years I have gone to thousands and given hundreds. And over the years I think I have been able to figure out what makes things work.

It seems to me that the best parties always combine the same elements. What I have tried to do here is to lay out those elements, starting with the point of the party, through invitations, the people, the food, the booze, the entertainment, and back to the point. Naturally, I've relied on my own experiences.

As a journalist it has been part of my job to meet a lot of interesting people both at work and at parties. Most of the people I write about here were our friends in the old days when we were having our "covered dish" spaghetti dinners, long before they became well-known.

Part of the reason I have included so many names here is because it is interesting to know that people, no matter who they are, how well-known or successful, or how much money they have, all have the same insecurities and make the same mistakes as everyone else.

So many people are needlessly puzzled and ill-at-ease about entertaining that they don't enjoy it. But there's really no need to feel that way.

There is no one right way to give a party, no perfect model.

I am hoping that seeing how I do it and what mistakes I've made along the way, what has worked and not worked for me and for others, will be helpful.

My parents are both from the South—my father, from the eastern shore of Maryland; my mother from Savannah, Georgia. I was brought up to believe in hospitality, and Southern hospitality in particular. My parents were brilliant hosts, no matter what their circumstances and who their guests were. They were brilliant because their primary concern was for their guests. They wanted everybody to have a good time, to have fun. They wanted people to feel welcome, and happy.

Once, years ago, when my father was in the army, stationed in Athens, Greece, my parents were invited to a dinner at the home of the ranking British admiral. It was very formal, black tie, with butlers behind every chair. There were cigarettes on the table (it was thirty years ago) and ashtrays. My father, who was a heavy smoker then, lit up after the main course, as was the custom. The admiral, a rather dour-looking man with a long face, leaned down toward my father, who was sitting at the other end next to his hostess, and said in a loud and reproachful voice, "General Quinn, in this house we do not smoke until after the sweet."

"Admiral," replied my father, leaning down toward his host, "in my house a guest can do no wrong."

That's it. The theory of entertaining.

A wonderful postscript: Several weeks later the admiral showed up at my parents' house for dinner and got so drunk he fell off his chair. Before the sweet.

Someone once asked Perle Mesta how she got so many famous people to come to her parties. It was very simple, she replied. All you had to do to get people to come to your parties was to "hang a lamb chop in the window." (Since then, in Washington, "hanging a lamb chop in the window" has become synonymous with simply having a party.)

She was being a little disingenuous. That might work for a while, but finally what will draw people back again and again is the feeling that the host and, yes, hostess really care about them and want them to enjoy themselves, regardless of whether the party is political, diplomatic, commercial, or just for fun.

What's wrong with that? What has been lost in the de-meaning of the word "host" or "hostess" is the fact that it is an honorable thing to be hospitable. I've decided that there are a lot worse things you can do in this world than to give people some good conversation, some good food and wine, some interesting and genial companions, pleasure, and a sense of well-being.

So you can call me a hostess anytime.

CHAPTER 1

The Point

The line for the palmist in the upstairs bedroom, which included the director of the CIA, formed at the bottom of the stairs.

There are a thousand reasons to have a party or to entertain, but as far as I'm concerned there is only one legitimate one. And that is to have a good time. If you don't care about having fun, then have a meeting.

I'm dead serious about this. The late Pamela Harriman, hostess and ambassador to France, once said that one should never have a party unless one had a serious agenda. That's ridiculous. A party is its own excuse, and the most successful way to further a "serious agenda" is to make sure all the guests enjoy themselves.

It is true that, in Washington, dinner parties have always had a special place in entertaining, mainly because they are often working events, no matter what the stated purpose. This must be true in New York or Chicago or Hollywood too, though not so easily recognized.

These dinners have always been a place where information and ideas are exchanged among the "power elite" of the capital. Henry Kissinger once wrote of Washingtonians that "it is at their dinner parties and receptions that the relationships are created without which the machinery of government would soon stalemate itself."

Translated, this means that people in different spheres need to get to know one another. But it doesn't mean they have to be bored to death doing it. Certainly people (not only in Washington but everywhere) have parties to further themselves professionally and socially. There's nothing new about that. What is important is how it is done. You have to be either extremely subtle or completely forthright about what you are doing. And you should actually like the people you are honoring or hosting, or you will soon earn a reputation for being a phony and a climber.

I once did a profile on a young would-be host, the late Steve Martindale, who was making quite a splash in Washington. He had recently had a party that both Alice Roosevelt Longworth and Henry Kissinger, then secretary of state, attended, and he had the rest of the town's A list as well.

How did he do it, this little unknown thirty-year-old from Pocatello, Idaho?

"Easy," he said. "I called up Alice Longworth and told her I was having a party for Henry Kissinger and then I called up Henry Kissinger and told him I was having a party for Alice Roosevelt Longworth."

Steve was a personable guy and was actually pretty good at it for a while, but he was just too obvious and it ruined him socially. It's never a good idea to be duplicitous. You always get found out in the end.

Years ago I found myself in a desolate situation. I had lost several jobs, broken up with my boyfriend, moved to California, been unhappy there, and moved back to Washington. I was living with my parents, and I was completely broke at age thirty. In other words, I had bottomed out. What was a girl to do?

Why, have a party.

Basically what I needed to do was announce that I was back in town and available for work. It so happened that Barry Goldwater Jr. had just been elected to Congress, and his parents were my parents' best friends. It was agreed by everyone that if I had a party for Barry Jr., who was attractive and fun, it would serve to introduce him to many of my friends in town and serve also as a sort of want ad for me. My parents bankrolled me. I sent out festive invitations to about two hundred of my "closest" friends, bought sexy one-shouldered white lace pajamas, and called the society columnists. (That's what they were called in those days. Sort of like "society hostess.") It turned out that the combination of Barry

Jr. and Barry Sr. was an irresistible draw. The columnists and photographers came in droves, the party was a huge success, and the next day I got a phone call.

"Hello," said this gravelly voice on the other end of the line. "Sally, you don't know me, but I'm Ben Bradlee and I would like to talk to you about a job at the *Washington Post*. Would you be interested?"

I was hired the next day. It seems that Ben had read the social columns and decided I was just the right person to cover parties for the newly created "Style" section.

So this party actually had two elements that I think are essential for success. It was great fun, and it had a reason, which I'll get to in a moment. The ostensible reason was to honor Barry Jr., but I have to say that I was pretty frank with my friends about the fact that it was essentially a job placement program for me as well.

Parties are usually more fun if there is a reason to have them. A "reason" is different from Pam Harriman's "serious agenda." Generally having a party just to have a party doesn't work as well as having a party for something or somebody. Even if you owe everybody in the world and have to have a payback party, you can always have it on or near a holiday or have it for a friend from out of town, just to give it a little more spark.

Actually, the only party I've ever had for no apparent reason was my own wedding reception. I had wanted a huge wedding with all the frills—twelve bridesmaids, flower girls, ring bearers, a beautiful dress with a six-foot train, a fabulous reception with at least three hundred people, the throwing of the bouquet, a limousine with a JUST MARRIED sign on the back, and a grand exit with rice being thrown as we headed for a romantic honeymoon destination. Ben did not. He had been married twice before and felt that it would be too much. Since we had been living together for five and a half years, I acquiesced, and we got married in a judge's chambers in Washington with only our immediate family and our attendants, *Washington Post* publisher Kay Graham as my matron of honor and, as best men, humorist and columnist Art Buchwald and lawyer Edward Bennett Williams.

I had arranged a small dinner party for about thirty or forty friends at our house afterward, with a wedding cake and white lilies everywhere. But Ben didn't want to tell anyone what the party was for beforehand because he didn't want to get scooped by the opposition newspaper, the *Washington Star*. (We were in a very competitive newspaper war.) This caused big problems for me because, as it turned out, Margaret and Peter Jay, the British ambassador and his wife, were having a dinner party that night and had invited us as well as half our friends. When I called everyone to invite them to "dinner," they all declined, and I had to coerce them into coming without revealing why. *What's it for? Who's the guest of honor?* they all wanted to know, and I was forced to demur. What I did was tell them in my sternest voice that I was calling in my chits, that this was extremely important and I wanted them to get out of the Jays' party and come to mine. They must have heard the resolve in my voice because they did it.

We had to contend with a number of grudging guests at the beginning of the evening, but once they saw the wedding cake and the white lilies everywhere, heard a few mushy toasts, and drank several glasses of champagne, they were mollified, and it turned out to be a wonderful evening. But I will never again have another party without an apparent reason.

P.S. We beat the *Star* on the wedding announcement.

Nobody really cares what the reason for a party is, but it does help to have one. You could have a Leap Year party and invite women and ask them to bring a man of their choice. That sounds silly, but it's already an amusing concept and there's nothing wrong with grown-ups being silly every now and then. I once had a Valentine's Day party in February (of course), when the weather and people's mood tend to be cold and dreary. Guests were greeted at the door with "love potions." God knows what was in them, but after about an hour men in black tie and women in evening dresses were reclining all over the living room floor giggling.

I got somebody to read palms and tell people about their love lives. Many of the guests were what you might call important and powerful Washington types, but the line for the palmist in the upstairs bedroom, which included the director of the CIA, formed at the bottom of the stairs. I could just as easily have had a regular dinner party, but it wouldn't have been nearly as much fun.

Having a party for no reason doesn't mean that people won't come. It's just that they usually can't figure out why they went in the first place. Two close journalist friends of mine, very much sought after as guests, recently went to a dinner party given by some newcomers who were clearly on the make. They complained bitterly to me afterward about what a tedious evening it had been.

"Well, why on earth did you go?" I asked them. They looked puzzled for a moment and finally one of them replied, "Because we were asked."

Talk about hanging a lamb chop in the window.

The point of the story, though, is that they will never go back.

There's always somebody you can have a party for, too. Someone writes a book (the book party has become the party of choice these days in Washington), has a birthday or anniversary, is leaving town or coming home, has just got a promotion . . . it gives the event a little more energy if there is a focus. I'm not talking here about having six or eight friends for dinner on a Saturday night. I'm really talking about larger dinner parties or cocktail parties or lunches or picnics. Whether it's a Memorial Day, Fourth of July, or Labor Day cookout, a Halloween, Thanksgiving, or Christmas party, a Valentine's Day or George Washington's Birthday bash,

Mardi Gras, an Easter egg hunt, or a May Day dance, everybody loves a reason to celebrate, and a party will be all the more festive if you give your guests a reason to do it.

We have a New Year's Eve party almost every year. It started about fifteen years ago when a group of us got tired of either having a forced New Year's Eve watching Guy Lombardo or going to bed at nine-thirty. The first year we had it at *Washington Post* columnist Richard Cohen's house. Richard's former wife, TV executive Barbara Cochran (then managing editor of the *Evening Star*), had everyone bring something (a covered-dish affair), and we all had a great time. The year after that we had bought our house in Georgetown and my friends voted to have it here. The Cohens' eleven-year-old son, Alex, played tapes for dancing. This was a disaster because he kept slipping in Prince records instead of golden oldies.

The following year Richard Cohen and British journalist Peter Pringle bought their first dinner jackets and insisted that the party be black tie since they thought they looked so sharp all dressed up. I hired a disc jockey. We were definitely going uptown.

Now the party has become such an event that I find I am competing with myself year after year. Every so often, when the pressure gets to be too much, we might decide not to have it. But that doesn't work either. Inevitably we find ourselves at our country house on New Year's Eve, just settling in by the fire with a tin of caviar and a bottle of champagne, when the phone starts ringing. One embittered former guest after another will call, some alone, some in pathetic little bands all around the country, looking for solace.

I figure we might as well go ahead and have the party. After all, it is for fun.

Even so, try to avoid having a party if you don't want to. It always shows when the host or hostess is put upon. If it's an engagement party for a friend who is marrying somebody you hate, or a dinner for your husband's or wife's new boss and all the boring people from the office, it's hard to get out of doing it. But it's better not to do it if you've got a chip on your shoulder, because if the host or hostess is not having a good time, nobody else will either. Every time I have grudgingly entertained, it has been a disaster. Why waste the time, energy, and money? Why not just take the engaged couple or the new boss and his wife out to one of your favorite restaurants for dinner? You may not have the best time of your life but you won't have had an awful party either.

I don't care whether you're organizing a charity event to thank donors, a corporate function for out-of-town personnel, or a baby shower for Aunt Lulu's horrible niece; there is still no excuse not to try to make it amusing. After all, that's the whole point. If you can't have a good time, forget it.

The only exception to having a social event that is not enjoyable is a funeral, and even then the guests should be made to feel as comfortable as possible. Actually, some of the most satisfying parties I've been to have been wakes or funerals where people tell funny stories about the departed and generally consume an enormous amount of booze. I'm planning to have a fun funeral myself, although I do hope that some tears are shed.

The best funeral I ever went to was for one of our closest friends, Larry Stern, the national editor of the *Washington Post*, who died of a heart attack while jogging, at age fifty. Though his many friends were in shock and grieving deeply, we managed a two-day wake that began at Nora's restaurant on Florida Avenue, moved to the Friends' meetinghouse across the street, and ended up on the eighth-floor garden court of the *Post* the next evening. After several hours of wonderful Stern stories, in the stifling August heat, my husband got up to deliver the final eulogy. When he was finished, he took his wineglass, which was conveniently on the lectern beside him, and hurled it against the brick wall. Instinctively, everyone else did the same. For several minutes, there was only the deafening noise of shattering glasses—a crescendo, a final few tinkles, then silence.

When it was over we filed out of the *Post* quietly and all went back to Nora's, where we continued our mournful revelry.

When the caterer's bill came for the glasses, some $337.84, Richard Cohen framed it and put it on the wall outside Ben's office along with a photograph of Larry.

Happily, nobody got hurt in the glass-throwing incident (Ralph Nader was there and was the only one concerned about the flying glass at the time), but I would definitely not recommend it. It did, however, lend a certain drama to the event.

Despite the fact that it was a funeral and we were sad, we all really had a good time in the right spirit for the right reason, mainly because all of us, all of Larry's friends, needed to be together.

CHAPTER 2

The
People

There is nobody alive who has not been to a Philadelphia rat fuck,
or P.R.F. It's like pornography. You can't really describe it, you just
know it when you see it.

If the reason to give a party is to have a good time, the most crucial element of a party is the people. The guests are everything —the beginning, the middle, and the end. If the guests are awful, the party's awful.

Obviously, different kinds of people work as guests for different kinds of parties, and there are occasions when you simply have to invite people you don't like or people who are deadly. Just try not to.

Weddings, christenings, graduations—with family parties it's really difficult to leave certain people out. The only thing you can do in those instances is try to work a little magic with the seating. Put the monosyllabic Joneses next to the Smiths who never shut up and hope they'll be happy at their table and won't realize why they're seated together.

Katharine Graham entertains a lot in Washington, flawlessly. She is often obliged to do official things. "Official things" means that certain people get asked because of their jobs, not their looks, charm, or personalities. If you're having a seated dinner, this can make things difficult, particularly if there are people invited whom you have never met.

Kay has sometimes prevailed upon me to help out in these situations by seating me next to an unknown person in the spirit of "family go light," or "family hold back" (the custom of having family members not eat too much if you're running out of food). But she has promised, "I'll always give you one really good person at dinner." My translation: the chances are you could have a dog as the other.

She has been true to her word. One night she gave me an attractive journalist on one side and a Japanese businessman who hardly spoke a word of English on the other. Fortunately, I had lived in Japan as a child, and though I don't speak Japanese, I do know many Japanese children's nursery rhymes. When I had finished my repertoire and he had finished nodding and smiling graciously and saying, "Ah so" (I'm sure he thought I was the dog), I turned and left him to Sen. John Heinz, on his other side, who struggled desperately the rest of the evening.

Another night I was at Kay's house for a business dinner for out-of-towners. There was a group conversation at our table and the subject of seating came up. I announced brightly the rule my hostess had for seating me at her house—one good person and one dog—when naturally a dead silence fell. To my horror I realized (what else could they do?) that each of my dinner partners was wondering whether or not he was the dog. My desperate assurances that I had drawn two winners this time was hardly credible. That may be my worst faux pas ever.

We all know people we are not crazy about. Some are people we work with, some we are related to, some are married to people we do like, and some just seem to be part of the community or group one sees all the time and can't really find a way to leave out. This creates a dilemma when you want everyone to have a great time.

My first instinct is always to say, well, I'll have a big cocktail party and work them all in. But that's tricky. Obviously, if you are having a large party and there is no seating, you can get away with inviting a few people with the personalities of an oyster. But not many. They form a critical mass faster than you can say "Bluepoint." If you get too many they will create a black hole at the party that will suck the life out of the rest of the guests.

I try very, very hard never to accept invitations from people I don't want to have back. Sometimes that's difficult if someone you're not wild about is having a party for somebody you love or are dying to meet, or everybody you know is going to be there. But

I basically think it's rude to go to someone's house if you never plan to reciprocate.

There are some ways to handle the situation if you have to invite people you don't like to your house. You can always have six or eight people for dinner or a barbecue or for a TV football game and supper. Invite some people who are mutual friends and who don't think the Warlocks are as bad as you do.

Wait. I just changed my mind. Life is too short. Why sit through a whole evening with the Warlocks? Remember, the whole point of entertaining is to have a good time. On second thought, work them into a large party, hope that they don't corner your prize guest and bore him to death, and forget it.

Speaking of prize guests, celebrities are always an interesting component of entertaining. Celebrities can be anything from the person in your hometown who foiled a robbery and ended up in the newspaper to the most famous movie star in the world. I mentioned earlier the importance of giving the party a focus, having a reason to entertain. Having somebody who has recently done something interesting gives the party an energy it might not have otherwise. Even the most famous celebrities love to meet other celebrities; interesting people like to meet other interesting people. There's hardly a person in the world who is so jaded that they don't like to meet people they've heard about, read about, or seen on TV or in the movies. This doesn't mean that you can't entertain without somebody famous. What you don't ever want to do is to invite people who are famous, or celebrities, that you don't like. It always ends up looking like you're stargazing and social climbing. People can just tell. If you don't really like your guests and don't care about them, or if you're just inviting them because they are big names, the atmosphere of the party changes from warm and welcoming to cold and calculating. And it makes you look bad.

It's fine to have a few people who stand out or are well known, but you don't want to get on overload, unless they know one another. One of the great untold secrets is that most White House parties are dull. I know this for a fact because I covered them for years for the *Washington Post*. For most people, simply being in the White House is exciting. What I'm talking about is, once you've gotten over the thrill of being there, the parties themselves usually aren't all that much fun. The reason they aren't really fun is that you have a whole lot of famous people from different professions and walks of life and none of them knows the others. So they all kind of stand around in little clumps and stare at one another, too shy to introduce themselves. I didn't realize this for years, until I was actually invited as a guest. I had always thought White House parties were great. That's because I was covering them. I had a notebook and pencil and I could just walk up to anyone, start a conversation, and ask them anything. Once, when Fred Astaire was a guest at a White House dinner, a group of reporters took a vote to see who would ask him to dance. An old-time news hen actually went up, tapped on his shoulder, and cut in on him.

When I finally did go to the White House as a guest for the first time, I took my father as my escort. My father is a gregarious Irishman who won't just stand around staring at the other guests. But even with his friendly introductions and my familiarity with the place, it was still pretty stiff. People simply find it difficult to relax at the White House. I don't know what the solution is, but when you have that many high-powered types who don't know one another, it never quite works.

The worst example of this I've ever witnessed was the shah of Iran's twenty-five-hundredth-anniversary celebration of his country, in a tented city in the desert outside of Shiraz. This extravaganza was held in the early seventies, and there must have been some fifty heads of state, kings, queens, emperors, princes, and assorted potentates. Aside from everything else, it was a protocol disaster, with everyone complaining that they were not being properly cared for. It's not possible to handle that many egos.

I was covering this for the *Washington Post* and happened to climb up into the rocks with a photographer to get some good shots of the tented city when I bumped into an extremely agitated Emperor Haile Selassie looking for his lost Chihuahua. He was only one of the many stars who was disgruntled at his host and hostess.

The worst part about the celebration was that everything, and I mean everything, was imported from Paris, including butter and, for the female guests, false eyelashes. There was nothing indigenous at the party, the sole purpose of which was to promote Iran.

Not only was this event the ultimate host-and-hostess nightmare; I honestly think that the outrageous extravagance of it actually contributed to the downfall of the shah and the takeover by Islamic fundamentalists.

I can't remember what the lesson is here . . . oh yes . . . don't overload your parties with too many celebrities.

In my first novel, *Regrets Only*, one of my characters is a Washington hostess called Lorraine Hadley. She is a professional social climber and she rates her guests at her parties by numbers, a five being the top guest, a one being the lowest. She tallies up all of her guests by rank, power, fame, and celebrity.

I made up this character, but there are always people who think this way, and it is the antithesis of really successful entertaining. I have never known anyone who could sustain this kind of party giving and naked ambition for any length of time. This kind of calculation is a guaranteed burnout, not only for the hostess but for the guests as well. And besides, no guest, regardless of rank, ever feels really good knowing he or she is being used.

One night years ago, Ben and his former wife arrived at a dinner party given by Alice Roosevelt Longworth. As they entered the foyer, they ran into a very powerful senator and his wife who were known to be on the make. "That's Ben Bradlee, the editor of

the *Washington Post,* and his wife," whispered the senator to his
wife. "You take him. I'll take her."

This is not to say that a celebrity or two doesn't liven things
up and quicken the pulse a little. And nobody in Washington can
deny the thrill of driving up to the front door of a party and seeing
the block cordoned off, police everywhere, vans, helicopters, am-
bulances, Secret Service, and marksmen on the roof—the tip-off
that the President is there.

I sometimes wonder whether or not certain hostesses have
hired guys in dark suits with earphones just to liven up their
parties.

The question often arises as to whether or not you should
invite people you don't know to your parties. One friend of mine,
no slouch as a Washington hostess herself, once remarked that she
always invited people she didn't know because she'd never meet
them otherwise. Certainly if you're having a party for someone
and they give you a list of friends, you invite them regardless of
whether or not you've ever met them. But sometimes, if there's
someone I'd like to meet or who sounds interesting, I just go ahead
and send them an invitation. I figure the worst that can happen is
that they will regret. Now, I don't do this unless I have a reason to
believe that they would like to come and that they would have a
good time. I don't do it often. And if they regret and don't ask us
back, I don't invite them again. You have to be careful not to
get a reputation as someone who just hangs a lamb chop in the
window.

I once went to a large party in East Hampton, New York,
with an enormous tent so packed with famous people you could
barely move. The host and hostess had clearly invited every well-
known person they had ever heard of. Half the guests didn't even
know the hosts, including us. Many of us had come because we
figured we could see our friends without having to host a party
ourselves. Everybody was making fun of the hosts. We met a lot of
interesting people but I never really was comfortable. The next

day I felt a little sleazy, as if I'd had a one-night stand with somebody whose name I couldn't remember.

There's a great story about the late Gwen Cafritz, when she was just getting started in the hostess biz years ago and was a little green in the social skills department. She was having a small cocktail party and called Congressman Joe Casey's wife, Constance, to invite them for drinks. Mrs. Casey replied that they would love to come. "I understand your husband has just been nominated to be secretary of labor," said Mrs. Cafritz. "That's right," replied Mrs. Casey. "Well," continued Mrs. Cafritz, "if he gets confirmed, we'd love to have you stay for dinner."

Wrong. Wrong. Wrong.

The most important thing you can do as a host or hostess is to make your guests feel comfortable, welcome, wanted. You must be thrilled to see them. They must believe that without them the party would not be the same. Establishing a comfort level is everything. I feel that way about my guests. Each person I invite adds something unique to my party. Hodding Carter, the journalist and commentator, has an incredibly tacky pair of plaid trousers, which he has had forever. He calls them his "drinking pants." Whenever Hodding walks in the door for a party and he's wearing his drinking pants, my heart leaps up and I know it's going to be a great party, even if he's on the wagon, which he always is for Lent. I try not to invite him during Lent, however.

Actually, Hodding's drinking pants are really a metaphor. Even when he's not wearing them, my heart leaps up when I see him. Each guest I invite has his or her own equivalent of drinking pants. There is something about each of them that makes me smile, that makes me delighted to see them.

I want my friends and my guests to take the same delight in one another that I do, which is why introductions are so important. I happen to think that it is really helpful when you're introducing people to tell them something about each other. I know there are those who think it is rude to define people by their jobs, but my feeling is that it is a huge waste of time to try to divine things about somebody when you could be having a lively and interesting conversation.

The Europeans and especially the British are always making fun of the way Americans introduce each other, listing off their curricula vitae as though they are applying for jobs. But I don't see it that way. What could possibly be wrong with saying, "This is Jane Doe. She has the prettiest garden in town, and is head of the Garden Club," or, "I want you to meet Tom Smith. He just had a piece on Russia in the paper last Sunday"? Think what a much better conversation they will now have instead of fumbling around commenting on the weather.

Sometimes, if people have important positions, it can sound a little like you are boasting as a hostess that you have big-deal guests. Get over it. They love to hear the sound of what they do; the people you introduce them to will feel excited to meet them; and the two of them will have a lot more to talk about than if you didn't. I recently had a small dinner for writer Calvin (Bud) Trillin and his wife, Alice, who were visiting from New York. The handsome young Czech ambassador (now chairman of the Czech senate's Committee on Foreign Affairs, Defense, and Security), Michael Zantovsky, was there, looking highly unlike an ambassador. As I introduced him and explained who he was, it turned out that several of the guests had just come back from Prague, had friends in common with him, or had some political interest in his country. One of the guests was a writer who had written about Woody Allen, and it turned out that the ambassador had himself once written a book on Woody Allen. That's right, the Czech ambassador. They could have groped around forever trying to find out what each other did, and it would have taken much longer for the party to get off the ground.

I try not to just ask people brazenly what they do if I get stuck without being introduced. For one thing, Europeans and a lot of

Americans find that question offensive. Usually I'll ask something like, "How do you know our hostess?" or, "Are you new in town?"

One of the problems with being too blunt is that the other person may have some very important job and have been written about every day in the paper, and you will look like a total imbecile for not knowing. That's why it's so charitable of the host or hostess to make introductions.

Another problem is that if the person you've just met is a woman who is at home with her children and doesn't have a career outside the house, it could be embarrassing or insulting. The most insulting thing a man can do is to turn to a woman and ask her what her husband does.

I actually had this happen to me before Ben and I were married, while I was covering the campaigns for the *Washington Post*. It was at a black-tie dinner at the National Gallery of Art, and my dinner partner was some out-of-town CEO of a major *Fortune* 500 company that had given a lot of money to the gallery.

He turned to me shortly after we sat down and said, "What does your husband do?"

"I'm not married," I replied.

His face fell. "Oh," he said, mustering up a sympathetic look as though I had just told him I was dying of cancer. "I'm so sorry."

I waited for the proper amount of time. Then I turned to him and asked sweetly, knowing full well the answer, "And what does your wife do?"

"Uh, well, um," he said, flushing. "She doesn't work."

"Oh," I said, lowering my head with an equally sympathetic look. "I'm so sorry."

With that I turned to my dinner partner on the other side and never looked back.

When I'm in a large group or in another city or there are people from out of town, I will always introduce myself by name, even if I'm pretty sure they know who I am. This is particularly helpful when you are meeting politicians or others who are introduced to hundreds of people every day.

I was once at a party on Capitol Hill talking to Jimmy Symington, who was quite a well known congressman, when this woman came up to him and said with a big grin on her face, "Hello. I'll bet you don't remember who I am!" Clearly he didn't have a clue, but because he didn't want to offend her, he slapped his forehead and kept saying, "Oh, wait a minute, I know I know you, it's right on the tip of my tongue. Of course I recognize you." It was especially painful, and the constituent seemed to enjoy seeing him squirm.

This is rude, hostile, and unacceptable. I learned a lesson that day. If anyone ever does that to me I just say, "You're right. I have no idea who you are. You'll have to help me out." It just wipes that sadistic little smile off their face.

However, this can backfire. There is a famous widow of a politician I've known for years and see once or twice a year at parties. Since we don't see each other often, I always introduce myself by name. Every time I do she grabs my arm and chastises me. "Oh, Sally," she says. "You don't need to introduce yourself to me. You must stop this. Of course I know who you are."

Finally, after years of this, I realized that she was getting annoyed, that somehow she must feel I was insinuating that she had lost her memory. So the next time I ran into her I held out my hand, gave her a big expectant smile, and said, "Hi."

Her face was a total blank as she reached her hand out to mine with a quizzical expression and introduced herself to me, clearly her way of letting me know she had no clue who I was and hoping to elicit my name.

These days, when women often keep their names after they get married, it can be confusing. If I don't know whether a woman likes to be called by her own name or her husband's, I simply ask, "How do you wish to be called?" Then I honor her request.

One of the rudest men I ever knew was the late Jack Kent Cooke, who owned the Washington Redskins. The Redskins had been partly owned by Ben's great friend Edward Bennett Williams. When Ben and I first got together we would go every Sunday to the football games and sit in the owners' box. Everyone would gather in the owners' lounge first for a drink, then head out to the box. It was great fun, very jolly and informal, everyone in jeans, with hot dogs and hamburgers and beer being served throughout the game. Then, when Cooke divorced his wife in California and paid her half his fortune, he moved East, took control of the Redskins, settled into the box—and a definite pall descended on us all. Suddenly there were waiters in black tie, linen tablecloths, petit fours, and fancy ladies from the hunt country in hats with long feathers in them. Definitely not our crowd. Shortly after Cooke invaded "our" box, Ben and I got married, and when Cooke introduced me to a guest as "Mrs. Bradlee," I good-naturedly explained to him that I had kept my own name.

"Nonsense!" he replied. "When a woman marries, she takes her husband's name, and that's all there is to it."

From then on, every Sunday, the minute we would arrive, he would grab my arm and try to drag me around the lounge to introduce me as "Mrs. Bradlee." I would wrestle free, smile, and say "Sally Quinn" as nicely as possible so as not to embarrass his other guests.

If it hadn't been for Ed Williams I would have stopped going to the games, Cooke was making it so unpleasant. But then I got my revenge. Cooke up and married a poor unsuspecting soul from Las Vegas, Miss Jeanne Williams. The first day that he brought her to the game after the wedding, I grabbed her, in front of him, and took her around and, not meaning to be rude, I couldn't resist introducing her to everyone as "Jack's new bride, Miss Williams."

He never called me Mrs. Bradlee again.

If you're the host or hostess and you're introducing your guests to one another and you forget somebody's name (I do this all the time; I have the memory of an ant), you have to wing it. I usually say, "But of course you two know each other," and then flee before they catch on that I don't have the foggiest. Luckily I'm famous for forgetting my best friend's name, so usually people don't get insulted. If anything, they're sympathetic. You usually see a look cross over their faces that says, "Thank God somebody else forgets names too." I can actually get away with saying things like, "I can't remember anyone's name here tonight. I just forgot my husband's, so you're on your own." Since that actually happened, I have credibility.

Obviously it's more difficult to remember names if you're having a huge cocktail party where you've invited everyone you've ever known and everyone you've ever owed. As we discussed earlier, this is not a great idea, but sometimes it's unavoidable, particularly if you rarely entertain and want to get it over with.

This sort of event has a name, coined by the late Marie Harriman, the dazzling second wife of statesman Averell Harriman. It is called a "Philadelphia rat fuck"—"P.R.F." or "rat fuck" for short. (This is definitely a challenge for the illustrator of this book.)

Marie used the term originally to describe debutante parties. She imported this expression to Washington, where it has been used over the years to describe half the events in this town. However, you may apply it to any event you can think of. There is nobody alive who has not been to a rat fuck, or P.R.F. It's like pornography. You can't really describe it, you just know it when you see it.

Here's the problem with having a P.R.F.: It's undiscriminating, and everybody knows it. You don't feel special for having been asked. And since the whole point of having a party is to make your guests feel special, it sort of defeats the purpose.

Sometimes I'm in the mood for large parties, but there are times I really enjoy just having dinner with six or eight people. If you're going to do a small dinner, though, it is crucial that the guests be compatible.

Alice Roosevelt Longworth, the legendary daughter of Teddy Roosevelt, took great pleasure in inviting people to her dinners who hated each other and then seating them next to each other. Then she would watch with glee as they either squirmed in discomfort or took out after each other. (She also had a needlepoint pillow in her drawing room that said, *If you haven't got anything nice to say about anyone, come and sit here by me.*)

I never did understand the point of that. It just seemed mean and sadistic to me. Remember the Golden Rule. I certainly don't want to be in the room with someone I intensely dislike, much less be seated next to that person. I want to relax and have a good time. So do most people unless they are perverse. Certainly you don't want people who agree on everything. That's boring, which is the ultimate sin in party giving. You definitely want spirited debate at the table. I always like it when my guests start throwing their napkins at one another. But it should be friendly and fun. You shouldn't, for instance, put a serious pro-choice person next to a determined pro-life person, or a spokesperson for PETA (the animal protection group) next to someone wearing a fur coat.

Toni and Jamie Goodale (she's a development consultant in New York; Jamie is a First Amendment lawyer) had a large book party for Ben a few years ago, and in walked, at the same time, Dan Rather and Connie Chung, who had just split up their CBS *Evening News* anchor team, as well as Judge Kimba Wood and writer Michael Kramer, who were in the midst of a very public divorce. Some of the guests, assuming that these people would not be speaking to one another, rushed up to Toni to advise her to separate them. As it turned out, they were all fine about it and it wasn't a problem. But it did remind me that people often agonize about their roles as host or hostess in these situations. My feeling is this: invite whom you want. If your guests are worried that somebody they don't like will be there, they don't have to come. If they find themselves arriving at the same time as somebody they're not speaking to, or in a room with someone they are uncomfortable with, let them work it out. That's not your problem.

Years ago I was planning a party in my old bachelorette apartment on California Street. I invited the writer Larry McMurtry and two women who were both interested in him and, unbeknownst to me, had had words with each other. One of the women, a close friend, told me that if I didn't uninvite the other she would never speak to me again. I did uninvite the other woman, reluctantly, and she has barely spoken to me since. And I don't blame her. We're all older and wiser now. I would never do that again.

I recently had a party where a guest was entering the front door and another guest, who had just been publicly fired by him, quietly whispered to me that he was leaving, and slipped out the kitchen door.

If you are among writers and journalists, you should be especially careful not to put a guest next to someone who has written something awful about him or her.

Sometimes, though, it's hard to know. Once, at a Swedish embassy lunch years ago, I was seated next to *New York Times* columnist Bill Safire, who had just written something that I considered negative about my husband. Of course, in high dudgeon, I turned my back on him and refused to speak to him the entire time. This was really awkward for everyone at the table, and I felt extremely bad about it. You can imagine, then, my chagrin when, after lunch, Ben came over to the table and threw his arm around Safire with a big friendly grin and a hearty "How are you, ole boy?" (Bill has since become an admired friend.)

So much for loyalty.

Ben and Kay Graham are very much alike on this score. Neither one of them is capable of carrying a grudge. Sometimes people will write bad things about Kay that upset her, and I don't speak to them for years. Then I'll go to her house for dinner and there they'll be, all bright-eyed and bushy-tailed, her new friends.

The question of whether or not to invite people who have been disgraced is always an issue. Maybe you don't know anyone who's been disgraced, but then you obviously don't live in Washington. Half the people here are publicly disgraced at some point in their careers for various reasons. My feeling is that your decision should be made on a case by case basis. How close are you to the person? Is the person somebody you need to stand up for, no matter what he or she did? Did the person actually commit a crime, or was the disgrace a little more personal, like getting caught with a prostitute, for instance, or having an affair, or being drunk and disorderly?

Oh, what is the poor hostess to do?

As always, the answer is simple. Do what you believe is the right thing to do, not what people think you should do. If the person has committed some crime and you basically believe that he or she is a truly decent human being who made a mistake, stand by your friend and invite him to your party. Have him next to you at the front door as you greet people, to show that you are supporting him. If your guests are offended, too bad. They can leave.

Unfortunately, too many people will weigh the consequences of their actions: Will this hurt me politically or socially? Could this person make a comeback and return to power? What will people think of me?

This is unfortunate. The only way people will respect you is if you do or say what you believe is right, and stick to your convictions. Even if people don't agree with you, they won't be able to disagree with the fact that you have stood up for what you believe in.

Some years ago there was a terrible scandal in Washington

when a well-known and socially prominent congressman was caught with a transvestite prostitute. The news was the subject of much titillation and gossip, but it was also greeted by friends of the congressman and his wife with great sadness because they were a well-liked and popular couple.

They went into seclusion while all of establishment Washington pondered how to handle the situation socially. Finally, one night, Joseph Alsop, the late columnist and Washington social arbiter, made the decision.

"There is only one thing to do," announced Alsop to his friends. "We must all have them to dinner."

The
Time

It's even trickier if the guests are the President and First Lady.

Defining the time of the party and limiting the number of hours are crucial.

My heart sinks when I get an invitation for an open house that reads, *Come anytime between 1 and 6,* or, *5 o'clock on . . .*

The thing is that you never know when to go. I like to be at a party when it reaches critical mass so I'll have a chance to see as many friends as possible. With these open-ended open houses it's a total crapshoot. You arrive at 3 P.M. figuring that's the middle of the party and find that all the people you wanted to talk to were there from one to two-thirty. Or you hear the next day that a whole group of fun people showed up just after you left . . . just after you left in desperation, having circled the buffet table twenty times, eaten too many ham biscuits, and had several endless conversations with the six foreign exchange students who happened to be the only guests there while you were.

I want to see *6:30 to 8:30 P.M.* on the invitation. Even six to nine is dicey because that's three hours from which to choose, and you're bound to miss a lot of people unless you show up at the beginning and stay until the bitter end. Basically I think that unless it's dinner or supper, a two-hour time limit is the safest guarantee that the party will be fun and the guests will have a good time. Besides, they always stay an hour later anyway, and three hours is enough for a cocktail party.

Invitations should be clear. There are all kinds of subtle and arcane little signals on invitations for the cognoscenti, but unless you go out a lot and get a lot of invitations, sometimes it's hard to know what in God's name the host or hostess is inviting you for.

At least, however, you should know the basics. "R.S.V.P." is from the French *Répondez, s'il vous plaît*—"Please respond." It means what it says. "Regrets Only" means you should respond only if you're not coming. "To Remind" means you've already been invited and this is a reminder. Often the French *Pour Memoire* is used instead of "To Remind." You don't have to do anything about that one except make sure the party is in your calendar.

I don't like to go anywhere in the evening before 6 P.M. I just don't feel like drinking earlier than that, so unless you're going on to some event later and have no choice, 6 P.M. is really the earliest you should start your party. That gives people time to get out of work and get to the party at a decent hour, or to go home and change if they feel grubby. I know people work later in Washington than they do in other communities. You just have to judge this by how you and your friends live. But anything that starts here before six is usually deadly for the first hour anyway, so it sort of defeats the purpose.

Here is what I think invitations mean or should mean.

If the party is 5 to 7 P.M. or five-thirty to seven-thirty, then the guest of honor or host and hostess probably have a later obligation. That means to me that they're going to be desperate to get you out of there on time. That means that already the totally embracing, welcoming atmosphere will be missing, which means you probably won't have a very good time. It also means a minimal amount of food (dips and chips, carrot sticks, and peanuts), since most people aren't really hungry at 5 P.M., and not too much booze either, since most people aren't ready to drink that early. For the host or hostess trying to save money, this may be the way to go.

Speaking of getting you out of there on time, it is always a difficult question how to handle guests who have regretted your dinner party because they have already accepted another invitation but would like to come by for drinks beforehand. What do you do when it's obvious that they find your party more fun than where they're headed and hang around after the time you've planned to serve? I would suggest that instead of telling them to leave or announcing dinner, thereby embarrassing them, you quietly say, "Are you sure you won't stay for dinner? We're about to go in."

It's a lot trickier if the guests are the President and First Lady. This happened recently to friends of mine here in Washington. They had a party for the writer Kati Marton, who was celebrating her birthday, and her husband, peace negotiator Richard Holbrooke. It was a Friday night, not a "school night" (where people have to get to work early the next morning), so there was a great group of people, and everybody was relaxed and up for a good time. The energy level was already high when people arrived at 8 P.M. to find President and Mrs. Clinton relaxing in the sitting room. The President was on crutches, as was Dick Holbrooke, and they had all obviously had a long and tiring day. It was clear from the beginning that the Clintons were unwinding and having a particularly good time, and everyone there was happy to be able to have a moment with them. With forty guests, including Secretary of State Madeleine Albright, PBS's Jim Lehrer and his wife, Kate, Vernon and Ann Jordan, and National Security Adviser Sandy Berger, it took a while for them to circulate and talk to everyone, and it was getting late. The hostess didn't have a soufflé that might fall, but as 10 P.M. approached, the President and First Lady were still there, the wine was flowing, and the party had definitely taken on a festive atmosphere. They had accepted for cocktails only but as time passed they were asked to stay, and only then did they realize the hour and beat a hasty retreat, leaving everyone basking in the glow.

Actually my fictional hostess Lorraine Hadley once remarked that the perfect party had the President and First Lady coming for cocktails and then leaving before dinner so that everyone could relax and talk about it for the rest of the evening.

Six to 8 P.M., or six-thirty to eight-thirty, means a good ole-fashioned cocktail party with passed hors d'oeuvres or food on the dining room tables or both, but it's basically picking food. Don't plan on staying past nine or nine-thirty. One hour past the invited

time is max. Some people get carried away when they have cocktail parties, and put on a big spread, but it's really not expected.
People should not plan on making it dinner. The exceptions to this
are things like big embassy National Day parties in Washington or
corporate events where you know there will be plenty of food. You
don't usually see plates at six-to-eight or six-thirty-to-eight-thirty
parties either.

At a book party we had for Kay Graham recently the invitation said 6:30 to 8:30. I had planned to have hors d'oeuvres passed,
plus food on the dining room table. But as the party approached I
began to get nervous when nobody was regretting and the numbers
were getting up there. By the day of the party we had two hundred
more people accepting than I had ever had in the house. I panicked, imagining crowds of hostile guests on the front door stoop
in the rain unable to get inside the packed house. So we took out
all the dining room furniture, including the table, which meant
only passed hors d'oeuvres. At one point in the evening, when it
was getting so crowded that people were holding their drinks above
their heads so as not to spill them, I was standing in the jammed,
emptied dining room when lawyer and Democratic insider John
Reilly appeared at the door and in a loud voice said, "What? No
food? Where's the food? You always have food!"

It was like a tiny dagger in my little hostess heart. I hardly
slept for the rest of the week, lying awake trying to figure out how
I could have accommodated the crowd and fed everyone well at
the same time—hanging platters from the chandeliers, maybe?
Needless to say, Ben slept like a log. I'm going to be Ben in my
next life.

Several years ago we had a book party for *Washington Post*
managing editor Bob Kaiser, and Pamela Harriman was a guest. At
one point Pam found herself talking to my mother, who was also a
guest. It was the summer and we had a very large group, which
had spread out over the porch and down into the garden. The
waiters were passing hors d'oeuvres, and after they had offered

some to my mother and Pam, Pam turned to her, unaware that she was my mother, and remarked, "I never pass hors d'oeuvres at my parties. I think it's so much nicer to have a large buffet table filled with food, and people can help themselves."

My mother simply smiled and walked away.

The fact is, particularly if you have a younger group who are hardworking and have families, that they want to come in, say hi, have a drink, do the room, have a quick bite, and be outta there. They don't want to stop and stand around a table for any length of time. Passing hors d'oeuvres just makes it easier and more efficient for them to see people, have some good conversations, a drink, and be on their way. A buffet table slows things down and diverts the crowd. I'm not saying that you shouldn't have a table with food, and I often do. All I'm saying is that no matter what, you should always have something passed as well, and if you have to choose, you should bag the buffet table.

Seven to 9 P.M., or six to nine. This is where it gets tricky.

I think anything past eight-thirty means you have to have plates and enough food so that people don't have to go home and cook or go out to a restaurant afterward. To me anything after eight-thirty means eats.

To avoid confusion, however, a host or hostess should put on the invitation what kind of event it is. Anything from 5 to 8:30 P.M. should be called a "cocktail party." If it goes after eight-thirty, it is a "cocktail buffet." You can call something earlier than that a cocktail buffet, but you have to mean it. That means plates. If you indicate 9 P.M. as the cutoff, the plates can be small, not regular dinner-sized plates. Anything after nine or no cutoff means big plates.

I have to tell you I get very bitter if I'm expecting a real meal and don't get it. Nothing annoys me more (or my husband, for that matter) than to have thought I was going to get fed and then going home, having had a couple of drinks, and having to forage around in the fridge for leftovers or some wilted lettuce to make a salad with. Ben usually ends up having another scotch and some fudge. I end up eating a piece of French bread, drinking a glass of wine, and going to bed in a bad mood.

Excuse the digression.

After 7 P.M. you can invite people for a "buffet supper." That means some sort of casserole and salad and cheese, at least, and there's no given time to leave. You can plan on making an evening of it.

Eight P.M. means "dinner," not supper, unless it's after an event or a performance that will be late, and then it's "supper."

For our New Year's Eve party (more on that later) I invite people for 9 P.M., just so people won't have to spend their lives waiting until midnight. We don't usually eat until ten-thirty, and I assume people will have had a snack earlier, so I serve a buffet supper. But that's obviously an unusual situation.

These things are not written in stone, but it helps to have some idea of what you're inviting people to and what they think they're being invited to.

As long as we're talking about timing, this is a good place to say that if you are having a large party or something that is important to you, it is always a good idea to check around town or with your newspaper's local events listing to make sure there isn't something else going on that might take away some or a lot of your guests. It's always depressing to send out invitations to something and then find out that the Children's Hospital or the Democratic or Republican National Committee or the Cancer Fund is having its annual event and half your friends are already going.

This happened to me when I was having a farewell party for Barry Goldwater after he retired from the Senate and was moving back to Arizona. Barry was a beloved figure in the Senate and I was pretty comfortable with the idea that most of his colleagues would come. But when he agreed on a date, apparently there was some confusion in his office and they didn't tell him that it was the night of some major Senate dinner. The problem was that most of the senators accepted, saying they would try to stop by for a drink on their way to the dinner. Unfortunately, there was a monsoon that night, with pouring rain and sleet making driving hazardous at best. I think only two senators showed up for a five-minute flyby on their way to the dinner.

It was pretty much a disaster, with a roomful of story-hungry journalists and no senators to feed off. Happily, Barry didn't seem to mind.

"Aw hell," he said, trying to make me feel better. "I see those bastards every day."

He was the center of attention, too, so from his point of view it worked out OK. I had a lot of food left over. And I vowed I would never again have a party without checking myself on what other events might be taking place the same night.

How late can you invite someone to a party and not make it seem as if they are an afterthought or a last-minute fill-in for somebody who dropped out?

Meg Greenfield, the editor of the *Washington Post* editorial page, has an ironclad rule that she will not accept any invitation after 7 P.M. for the same evening. A more relaxed Barbara Howar says she will accept up until the first course is served. But she lives in California.

My feeling is this: know your friends. I have many friends who entertain, and we all know one another well and don't expect to be invited to every party. If one of them is having a dinner for her boss and suddenly has a dropout and needs us, and we're free, I'll go happily and not be offended. If, however, she is having a party for the queen of England and everyone in town is invited except for me, and she calls at the last minute because she has an empty seat, I will definitely not be happy about it.

The point is that you want to make people feel good. If they end up hurt or insulted or feeling used to further your social advancement, that defeats the whole purpose of entertaining, doesn't it?

It helps to tell people what to wear. People feel very insecure if they don't have a clue what others will be wearing. If you're from out of town it's probably a good idea to ask your hostess what to wear because styles of dress differ from community to community.

"Informal" usually means a suit for men and a suit or dress for women.

"Black tie" means dinner jackets for men and, depending on the event, long or short evening outfits for women.

"White tie" means white tie and tails for the men and long dresses for the women. "White tie with decorations" means stay home.

All this is moot in L.A., where people wear anything they want. Washington is much more careful. New York is more businesslike.

Basically, for women, one good-looking black suit will go anywhere. Period.

The kiss of death is "Black tie optional." That's not fair. Either it's black tie or it's not. Either it's formal or it's not. I have no idea what it means, and it sounds like the host or hostess doesn't either. It also sounds like they don't think enough about their guests to make them feel comfortable by telling them what is expected. My view is that if the invitation says *Black tie optional* it means that they don't think the event is special enough to warrant black tie. If they don't think so, neither do I. Men should wear a dark suit and women should wear a short something or pants.

When you're sending out invitations, do you buy blank invitations and write out everything? Do you buy the fill-in-the-blank kind—*Blank invites you to a blank on the blank of . . .* , and so forth?

Do you have invitations printed or engraved? And if so, do you have the ones engraved with just your name, and fill in the blanks? Do you call, and if so, do you send a reminder? Do you fax?

It can get very complicated.

The fact is, I don't think there is one good answer, which means I don't know. I have done all of the above.

For a few very special occasions I have had invitations engraved. But it's very expensive and I don't think most people expect it unless it's a wedding, a big birthday, a significant anniversary, or something like that.

Occasionally I'll have fancy invitations printed up. That's fine too. Sometimes I've gotten the ecru fill-in-the-blank ones from the stationery store. But frankly I find it works better for smaller parties to call and for larger ones to fax everybody. The problem with invitations is that they get lost in the mail, people move, and you think of new people to invite as the party date approaches.

One New Year's Eve party I had beautiful gold-and-white invitations printed up and sent out. It was a nightmare. At least twenty percent got lost. And we had to get on the phone and start calling everyone we hadn't heard from. Half the invitations went to offices where the secretaries would open them and type up the schedule, and the invited guests never even saw them. I vowed never again.

This year everyone got a fax and a phone call. I thought it was an unbelievably tacky thing to do, but it was by far the most efficient.

I will say, however, that Tony Kornheiser, noted sports columnist and radio and TV commentator, invited for the first time to our New Year's Eve party, got the fax and called Carol Leggett, Ben's secretary, immediately.

"That's it?" he bellowed into the phone. "That's it? All these years I've been hearing about this fabulous party, and all I get is this dumb fax?"

Never mind! When he was last seen it was midnight and he was sprawled on the living room floor, champagne in hand, shrieking "Hap-py New Year" to anyone who would listen.

I love getting festive or original invitations in the mail. It's so much fun to open them. (Skip the confetti in invitations. I consider it a hostile act. Just try sweeping up all those ridiculous bits of colored paper off the floor.) And I always admire the people who have the fortitude, time, energy, and creativity to deal with great invitations. I do think that, in some ways, an invitation can set the mood for the whole party and show the guests that you are prepared to make an effort for them. If only the postal service made the same effort.

In the end, though, the thing that matters is whether everyone has a good time. Remember, it's the people, not the invitations, that count.

CHAPTER 4

The
Anxiety

"This party is boring, boring, boring."

When my son, Quinn, was four years old I had a birthday party for him in our backyard. I invited many of my friends and their children. We had hot dogs and hamburgers and pink lemonade, and I hired a clown to do tricks and make animal balloons. We had a huge chocolate birthday cake, and ice cream with sprinkles, and lots of goody bags. I thought I had done everything possible to make this a great party. Shortly after the cake and ice cream, I was walking across the lawn when I overheard two six-year-old girls talking. One of them turned to the other, her curls bouncing, put her hands on her hips, and with what I can only call a sneer pronounced, "This party is boring, boring, boring."

I died. Tears welled up in my eyes and I barely made it into the house before I burst out crying. This was every hostess's nightmare—only worse, because I had obviously humiliated my child and he would never recover socially from his mother's incompetence. I would never entertain again. I was devastated.

I've never known anyone who hasn't had some kind of bad experience with a party. This is why there are so many people who are terrified to entertain. What if the guests don't have a good time, what if the food is terrible, what if something awful or embarrassing happens? You can make yourself crazy with this kind of thinking. Don't. If you think that way, you never will entertain again, and that would be too bad.

In one of my earlier birthday parties for Ben, in East Hampton, Long Island, in August, we invited about sixteen people for dinner. I had gone to considerable trouble. So when the weather bureau announced hurricane warnings that morning I couldn't decide whether to be more upset about my party being canceled or the possibility of my house being destroyed. Guests were on the phone all day comparing notes about the weather. Though it did look like we were in for a big storm, it wasn't supposed to hit until much later, so my party-mad friends all decided to brave the elements and come anyway. Dick Cavett drove all the way from Montauk with his dog in the car, Swedish actress Bibi Andersson was there, as were Tony Award winner Peter Stone (*Will Rogers Follies, Titanic, 1776*) and his wife, Mary. Ben had put plywood boards across some of the sliding glass doors and we all hunkered down with plenty of liquor to anesthetize us in case we were blown away with the house. The sound of the wind and crashing trees provided Peter and Dick with plenty of material for their running black humor. Naturally, the hurricane dominated the entire evening, and the possibility, though slight (very slight, actually), that we might not survive brought us all closer together. Plus the booze. What started out as a potential disaster of an evening ended up being one of the better and more memorable parties we've ever had. The experience was heightened, too, by the fact that we all lived to tell about it.

    Ask any veteran Washington host or hostess and they will tell you how the great parties, the perfect parties, always take place on the night of a crisis. Of course, here, "great" or "perfect" may simply translate into memorable or legendary, which means historic which means important.

    Often a "memorable" party means that something awful or tragic happened but after a while people forgot that it ruined the party and remember only that it was an incredible evening and then it becomes part of the legend.

Here are three stories of parties that can now be labeled memorable for that very reason. Though these events were televised all over the country, in Washington they actually caused the parties to break up because of the number of journalists and/or members of the administration who were there.

In the spring of 1968 Warren Hoge and I decided to have a party at the house Warren shared with two other guys, right off Pennsylvania Avenue, several blocks from the White House. At the time Warren was the White House correspondent for the *New York Post*, covering President Lyndon Johnson. (He is now the London bureau chief of the *New York Times*.)

We invited a large number of journalists (many of whom covered the White House with Warren), cooked up a big pot of jambalaya, laid on plenty of beer and wine, and were prepared to welcome our guests. However, at the last minute the White House announced that the President would be addressing the nation that evening.

The White House had released a copy of the President's speech that day and it was relatively bland with not much news in it. After a number of phone calls, many of the reporters who were covering the White House decided to write the story before the speech was delivered, watch the speech from our house in case there were any last-minute changes, and phone in corrections to the desk. Warren, who worked for an evening newspaper, made the same decision, knowing that he would miss his paper's deadline anyway and would be filing for the next day's afternoon paper.

After a few drinks, we switched on the TV, everyone quieted down, and, with copies of the President's speech in hand, people listened and took notes while he spoke. But then, to the horror of many of the reporters there, Johnson announced that he would not run for another term. Panic is not the word for what ensued. There were several near murders as everyone grabbed for the one phone in the house, and when people realized they couldn't all use it at once, many of our guests, including Warren himself, left the house and literally ran all the way to the White House.

That was pretty much the end of the party, except for the few nonjournalists left to make a dent in the jambalaya. But to this day I still have people come up to me and remind me of that "great" party Warren and I had the night Johnson dropped out of the race.

Five years later, in the fall of 1973, in the middle of Watergate, Art Buchwald had a party/tennis tournament at an indoor tennis court in Arlington, Virginia. Half the administration was at the party, and people were playing tennis, drinking, eating, and having a great time when, one by one, the government officials and journalists were summoned from the courts to the phones. Finally it became clear a major story was unfolding. It was the Saturday-night massacre, the night President Nixon forced Solicitor General Robert Bork to fire special prosecutor Archibald Cox after Attorney General Elliot Richardson and his deputy, Bill Ruckelshaus, had both quit rather than fire him themselves. This event totally disrupted the party even though it gave everyone something to talk about. Ben and I had stayed away from the party because we had just recently gotten together. I was still the coanchor of the CBS Morning News in New York, our romance had been something of a scandal, and we weren't yet ready to make our first public appearance together.

The interesting thing about that evening was that Ben and I had had dinner at our then-favorite restaurant, Chez Camille, with Barbara Howar and the writer Willie Morris. The waiter brought a phone to the table when the story broke, and Ben had to head back to the paper. But over twenty years later, when Ben was writing his memoirs, he wrote about Artie's party and said that we were there. Only after I read the first draft of his book and saw his mistake did he realize what he had done. He had heard so much about the party afterward that he thought he remembered having been there!

So you see what I mean about memorable parties.

Sometimes a terrible tragedy will mark a party as one to be remembered. This happened to us in July of 1993.

That night I had a large seated dinner for forty-eight at our house for *New Yorker* media writer Ken Auletta with a lot of administration people there. I had half of the guests in the dining room and half in the connecting library. It was great fun, very jolly, and we were all enjoying ourselves when, as dessert was being served, the telephone in the library rang and the President's communications advisor, David Gergen, was summoned to the phone. Looking very grim, he came back from the phone and went around the room seeking out various other members of the administration and friends: Mickey Kantor, the trade representative; James Carville, the President's campaign manager; Vernon Jordan, his informal advisor; Les Aspin, the secretary of defense; Roger Altman, deputy secretary of the treasury. They all convened in the hall, and I can't begin to describe the total desperation of the journalists left behind.

Clearly there was some crisis of national security with all the White House people out in the hall, and the reporters—Johnny Apple of the *New York Times*, Al Hunt of the *Wall Street Journal*, Walter Pincus of the *Washington Post*, and Evan Thomas of *Newsweek*—began getting up and milling around nervously, comparing notes with one another, one eye on the hall.

Then the administration types started heading off for various phones, and there was a near riot as the reporters, not being able to stand it another minute, began hounding those who were still in the hall.

Finally Gergen could hold out no longer. Vince Foster had

committed suicide. It was Mark Gearan, one of the President's assistants, who had called him with the news and to say that the President had been told during a commercial break on the Larry King show and had just left the studio.

A hush fell over the library as one after the other whispered it around and the horror of what had happened began to sink in. I was in the dining room, unaware of what had ensued as there was still a considerable amount of good-natured joshing and speculating and hilarity going on.

Finally someone from the library came in and filled me in. I immediately stood up and went out into the hall to join those who had gathered there. The dinner was definitely over.

After several minutes of quiet condolences to those who were friends of the Fosters, everyone left.

A week or so later Meg Greenfield, who was also a guest that night, wrote a column in which she described the events of the party, without using our names, and talked about how tragic yet how dramatic the evening had been.

Some weeks after that, I was doing the Charlie Rose show with several other Washington types when Charlie suddenly turned to me and said that he understood there had been a party in Georgetown the night of Vince Foster's death, and had I by any chance been there? Stunned, I replied that yes, as a matter of fact it had taken place at my house. I was embarrassed because I didn't want to be seen as trying to capitalize on the tragedy, but I didn't know how else to respond. (Later one of the New York gossip columns reported "Sally Quinn appeared on the Charlie Rose show and was eager to let the world know that the dinner was held at no less an august place than the Georgetown residence of . . . Quinn and husband Ben Bradlee.")

This was just another example of how a party becomes legendary in Washington, not despite, but because of, some catastrophe occurring. That party at our house is now referred to around town, years later, tasteless though it may be, as the "Vince Foster Party."

Sometimes as a host or hostess you are faced with a situation that at first seems anxiety making because it could be disruptive or go against your carefully laid plans. This is especially difficult for perfectionists and control freaks, neither of which I am, though I'm sure my husband would disagree.

What I'm saying here is that sometimes it is necessary to go with the flow. You've got to be prepared to change your plans, add a seat or take away a seat at the last minute. You have got to be flexible or you will never be any good as a host or hostess. And besides, often a party will end up being more fun than you had actually anticipated if things don't go exactly as scheduled.

This happened to me recently when we were having a dinner for eight for actor-director Rob Reiner. After we had scheduled the dinner I realized that it was the night of the President's State of the Union address, February 4, 1997. That was fine, I thought; we would just eat early in the dining room and then have dessert at nine in the library in front of the TV set.

However, when Rob and the other guests arrived, they were on fire because the O. J. Simpson jury was due to come back with the verdict on the civil trial. We turned on the television immediately and were all riveted to the screen. It was clear that nobody wanted to turn off the TV, so what I did was set up a buffet, and during a lull around eight-thirty we all went in to eat, with the door to the library open and the TV on. Guests would get up and walk in and out of the room depending on what was going on on the screen. Then, when it was time for dessert, we had it in the library. Rob, it turned out, because he lives in Los Angeles, was an expert on the O.J. story and had a lot to add to what was going on. The evening ended up being exciting and

electric, really because of the "double feature" on television—
which it would not have been if I had turned off the TV and
insisted that everyone go into the dining room. Apparently there
were several other parties around town that evening where the
hosts insisted on doing just that. But it seems to me that that
would destroy the whole purpose of the party, which is . . . lest we
ever forget . . . to make sure the guests have a great time.

To entertain well you have to be an optimist or at least a
realist. Sometimes things go wrong, so you go with the flow. Sometimes when things go wrong it actually makes the party better
because people identify with you, and that makes them relax and
be more comfortable. A there-but-for-the-grace-of-God-go-I sort
of thing. Nothing like a little schadenfreude to give a party a lift.

Oddly enough, I have never really been nervous about a party
except for parties for Quinn. I started dreading his birthday six
months beforehand. I actually did a huge party for him every year
until this year, when he turned fifteen and I couldn't handle the
stress anymore. You'd think I would have had the sense to bail out
earlier.

For his thirteenth birthday I planned a big bash, for about
eighty people, and I hired a DJ who specialized in teenage parties,
someone who knew all the right games and party dances and
things. I served hot dogs and pizzas, but the kids were asked to
wear party dresses and coats and ties. It was the first really
grown-up party many of them had been to.

I started drinking shortly before the party began, 7 P.M. By
eight o'clock I was half in the bag. About eight-thirty I sneaked
inside the house (the party was outside) just to take a break from
the tension and to make another trip to the bar. (We had no booze
outside.) One of the waiters I had hired caught me guzzling a glass
of wine.

"I can't believe this," he said. "I've worked at so many of your parties where there have been really amazing people, and you always seem so calm. But tonight you are a total wreck and there are only a bunch of thirteen-year-olds. What's the problem?"

That was a seminal question. Remember what I said earlier about how people are the most important ingredient? The problem, I finally figured out, was that because I didn't know many of the children, I had no confidence in how they would react. All I could think of was Quinn's fourth birthday party and "boring, boring, boring."

It occurred to me afterward that the reason I don't get nervous at parties with my friends is exactly that. They're my friends. I like them, they like me, and we are all full of goodwill for one another before the party. Everyone wants to have a good time and, even more important, expects to have a good time, and I know they will make every effort.

The kiss of death for any party is a hostess who is a nervous wreck. We've all seen the exhausted, overwrought hostess who greets you at the door as if you're coming to a funeral. She's hyperventilating, rushing around pushing you from group to group —come here, go there, have a drink, you-must-try-these-hors-d'oeuvres-I-was-up-all-night-making-them kind of thing.

When I see one of these hostesses (or hosts, for that matter), I always wonder why on earth they would want to put themselves through anything as painful as it obviously is for them to have a party. But more than that, I just want to shake them and shout, *"Stop thinking about yourself. Think about your guests."*

It's the same feeling I have when I hear people talking about how shy they are. It just seems to me that if you concentrate on the other person and try to make him or her feel comfortable, you'll forget your own insecurities. It falls into the "Do unto others" category, which, after all, is what parties should be about.

Probably the most legendary moment of hostess anxiety that

anyone can remember happened right here in Washington, D.C., at the Canadian embassy in 1986.

Allan and Sondra Gotlieb, the Canadian ambassador and his wife, had been in Washington for several years. They had almost single-handedly revived Embassy Row, which had been virtually moribund since the Six Day War shut down party-giving at Arab embassies, in 1967. Their parties were fun and they always managed to pull in the power crowd, the congressional and administrative figures as well as the journalists.

One evening the Gotliebs were having a large party for Canadian prime minister Brian Mulroney and *le tout* Washington (everyone) was invited. Vice President George Bush was running late, so Sondra Gotlieb suggested that we all begin moving out to the garden, where tables had been placed on top of a boarded-over swimming pool for the night. (This is very risky. I was at the deep end and never drew a relaxed breath all night.) Sondra seemed particularly agitated as she headed for the front door and took her place outside on the steps to wait for the Bushes while we were all being seated outside. Unfortunately the entire press corps was stationed in the driveway also awaiting the arrival of the vice president.

As she stood there she turned to her social secretary and asked what had happened to Richard Darman, Reagan's assistant treasury secretary and much-sought-after guest. When her social secretary informed her that Darman had dropped out at the last minute, an overwrought Gotlieb slapped her across the face, in full view of the hordes of reporters and photographers.

Needless to say, the story made the next morning's papers. Those of us who were there were stunned to have to learn about it in the paper (it's much more fun to be the first to know). Sondra Gotlieb's career as a successful Washington hostess was, as we say in the nation's capital, history.

The thing to remember is that everyone has insecurities, and if you concentrate on that fact it will help you to feel more secure yourself. And think about the advice often given to first-time public speakers: imagine everyone you're speaking to is sitting there naked.

A friend of mine who gives great parties announced facetiously several years ago that it helped her feel calmer if she thought of herself as a hospice worker and her guests as dying patients she had to minister to. I thought that was a rather macabre way to look at it, but whatever works, I suppose.

The most instructive example of how thinking about your guests eases your own anxiety was a party Ben and I had the night our son, Quinn, had open-heart surgery, when he was three months old. I know that sentence is a shocker. The idea of it was to me, too.

Quinn had been admitted to Children's Hospital in Washington six weeks earlier in heart failure, and I had been living at the hospital with him, never leaving him for a night. Quinn went in on a Sunday. On the following Monday the *Washington Post* went to trial in a very high-profile libel suit brought by Mobil Oil Corporation against the *Post*, Ben, author and investigative reporter Bob Woodward, and another reporter, Patrick Tyler. Ben had to be in court all day every day. He would begin his day at the hospital with Quinn and me, spend the main part of the day in court, and then join Quinn and me at night in the hospital, staying until it was bedtime. We were both exhausted and obviously under enormous stress as the day neared when, the doctors had decided, Quinn had to have surgery. The night before his surgery I didn't sleep. He wasn't allowed food and therefore couldn't nurse, so I couldn't hold him and he cried all night. By the day of the surgery I was a complete basket case.

We spent most of the morning and early afternoon waiting

while Quinn was being operated on, joined by Kay Graham and Ed Williams, his godfather. When the surgery was successfully completed and Quinn was in the recovery room, Ben left to go back to court for the verdict, only to learn that the jury had found against the *Washington Post*. He left the court and came back to the hospital, where Quinn was being moved into the intensive care unit.

The doctors had assured us that Quinn was doing beautifully, and they told us that there was no place for the parents to sleep there, that we couldn't stay in intensive care. They advised us to go home and get some rest. We decided to stay until about 8 P.M. and then go home. It was then that Ben suggested that we have a party to thank everyone from the trial. We invited the lawyers, David Kendall (now the Clintons' lawyer) and Irving Younger; the reporters, Woodward and Tyler; and the editors and everyone's wives to come to our house for carryout Chinese food. I was so shell-shocked by the day's events that I just nodded.

We ended up with twenty or twenty-five people at the house. I barely had time to take a shower and change before they arrived. There was plenty of wine and beer and scotch, and cartons of Chinese food that Ben's secretary had ordered. Everyone was devastated by the verdict and needed cheering up, and without even thinking I went right into my Savannah, Georgia, Southern-hospitality hostess mode. I suddenly became preoccupied with making my guests feel good—Is there enough to eat? How about another drink? Sit here, it's more comfortable. Tell me about the trial; oh, isn't it awful?—and miracle of miracles, I forgot for a few hours what absolute hell I had been living in for the last six weeks. Trying to take care of and nurture my guests had taken my mind off myself and what Quinn and we had been through that day. When I finally did go to bed I was able to relax and get the first good night's sleep since he had been born, three months earlier.

When we got to the hospital the next day he was doing wonderfully well; he was out of intensive care the next day, and home in six days! It took a lot longer for the libel case to be resolved, but several years later the Supreme Court ruled in our favor.

Every now and then, when Ben and I remember the fact that we had a party that night, we shake our heads in wonder. What were we thinking of? It was preposterous, really. And yet, in the end, it was therapeutic for everyone and particularly for us, simply concentrating on making sure that our guests were well taken care of.

At a dinner party at Katharine Graham's several years ago, the room was filled with important and powerful people and I was seated next to one of them, a man who is one of the richest men in the world.

We began talking and I started asking him questions about himself. This, by the way, is one of the great benefits of being a reporter. I am curious about everyone. Even the most seemingly boring person has a story to tell if you dig deep enough. When conversation lags it never fails to actually try and interview somebody. It's incredible how open people will be and how flattered they are if they think you are really interested in them.

It seems that this extraordinarily rich, powerful, and famous man, a Rockefeller, had been terribly insecure as a child, had no confidence in himself while growing up, and still felt that way. It was an ordeal, he admitted to me, even now, in his late middle age, to walk into a dinner like the one we were attending and have to greet all the important and famous people there. I was astonished to hear him talk this way and asked him how he managed to overcome his insecurity enough to function socially in groups like these.

"Well," he said, "I have this little ditty my governess taught me as a child, which I sing to myself under my breath whenever I enter a room full of people. It goes like this," and he began singing in a lilting childlike voice: "Everybody loves me, nobody hates me, everybody loves me, nobody hates me . . ."

I don't think I've ever been more flabbergasted in my life, listening to this man so many people were in awe of singing his touching little song to me that night at dinner. What I did learn was that you must always assume that you are not the only one who has self-doubts, and as a host or hostess you must try to make everyone feel as though "everyone loves them, nobody hates them."

There is something interesting about anxiety. It is catching. If you're anxious, others will be too. If you're calm and secure, others will pick up on that. It's almost like an animal scent, the scent of the jungle. You can spot it immediately at parties—the alpha males who come in and are immediately surrounded by other men, who have picked up on their scent of confidence and strength and energy. You can see it with women, too, who exude a kind of sex appeal even when they aren't young and beautiful. So much of what they are putting out is an attitude about themselves, what they think of themselves.

I once had a dance teacher at Smith College who used to say that how you carry yourself into a room is everything. It will determine completely what people think of you. Then she would imitate someone walking into a room with shoulders hunched over, creeping sort of sideways, looking pathetic and as if they should apologize for being alive. Next she would pull herself up, and with ramrod posture, her chin up, her chest out, her head held high, she would march straightforwardly into the room as though she owned it. It was a vivid image that made an incredible impression on me and stays with me still. "What you think of yourself," she would say, "determines what others think of you. If you think you're worthless, others will say, well, she ought to know!"

There's a wonderful story, which may be apocryphal, of Marilyn Monroe walking down Fifth Avenue in New York with a friend. The friend was stunned that nobody seemed to recognize Monroe and remarked to her how surprising it was. Monroe turned to her companion and asked if she would like to see her become Marilyn Monroe. The friend said yes, at which point the actress pulled herself up, tossed back her hair, pouted her lips, stuck out her chest, and began sashaying down the street. She was recognized instantly and, within minutes, so besieged by fans that the police had to be called.

This is just an example of how you can create an aura of confidence simply by improving your posture and your demeanor.

Walter (Fritz) Mondale, who lost his bid for the presidency, reportedly commented to a colleague afterward that he had to leave Washington because he couldn't bear running into people at parties who treated him as a loser. "I can see it in their eyes," he supposedly told his friend.

It interested me because this man was greatly admired by most people in town—even journalists, which is saying a lot— and people were always happy to see him and invite him to their parties. I suspect it was his own attitude about himself at the time —that he thought he was a loser—that made him think everyone else would treat him as one.

On the other hand, you see someone like Gen. Colin Powell. He retired from the army and hasn't had an official job since, yet he is treated like a hero and a major celebrity at every social event he attends. His expectations are that people will deal with him as they did before because he is still the same person. The brass on his shoulders was not what made him.

I've mentioned scandals earlier—how to handle the situation when friends get caught up in one. Whether you are a guest or a host or hostess, the same thing about confidence applies. When screenwriter-director Nora Ephron's husband, journalist Carl Bernstein, had an affair with Margaret Jay, the wife of British ambassador Peter Jay, it was a huge scandal, very public, in all the papers and magazines. But Margaret Jay didn't leave her husband right away. Instead of cowering at home to avoid seeing people, she and her husband, the ambassador, were out on the party circuit every night. At first people were hesitant to invite them because they didn't know what to say. But the Jays seemed so self-assured, almost defying people to mention the affair or treat them with any disrespect, that soon they were being asked everywhere and people were treating them as they always had.

The moral of all these stories: people see you the way you see yourself. If you are a confident host or hostess, people will relax and have a good time. If you're a nervous wreck, you'll give off those vibes, the guests will pick up on them, and they won't feel comfortable either. It's catching.

Aside from the people you invite, the most important aspect of entertaining with confidence is never to entertain beyond your means. If you're the queen of England you can have butlers in tails and white gloves behind every chair. If you live in a cottage or a log cabin, that just won't fly. It would be pretentious and silly. If you live in a cottage, have a cookout or invite people over for a fried chicken dinner. If you live in a log cabin, have barbecue or a big stew or venison steaks. If you live in a mansion, you can have finger bowls and five courses and lots of waiters, if you're used to that. The point is that you don't want to try to entertain in a way that is completely foreign to the way you live. Tom and Meredith Brokaw have an apartment in New York where they entertain elegantly. They also have a ranch in Montana with a couple of tiny log cabins and two modest cottages. When they entertain there, everyone wears jeans and it's strictly homestyle, with simple, delicious food, buffalo steaks, bowls of vegetables, and potatoes passed around the table. It's very informal and great fun. The point is each place is very different, and the way they entertain for each place is different and appropriate. Obviously, if you're having a seated dinner for thirty and you usually eat in the kitchen or family room, you would have to do things a little more formally than normal. Or if you're doing a huge thing like a wedding or large anniversary party with a tent and lots of people, you would do that differently too. What I'm talking about is that you shouldn't try to be something or somebody you are not. Your guests will be the first to notice. You will be anxious, and so will they.

When I'm flying I'm always a wreck, partly because I get so exhausted keeping the plane in the air. When I'm at a party where the host or hostess is nervous, I feel like I do when I'm flying: somehow I've got to keep the party alive or it will crash and burn. It's exhausting. You don't want to do that to your guests. It's not what you would want them to do unto you.

Finally, one sure way to avoid being anxious is to be prepared. If you know what your menu is, if you have prepared as much as you can in advance, and if you've got enough booze, flowers, and candles (we'll get to details on all this later), then that's really all you need to worry about.

Just put on a happy face, stop thinking about yourself, and concentrate on making sure your guests have the best time they've ever had.

There is one hostess-anxiety problem I haven't solved. It's a form of posttraumatic stress syndrome. I have experienced this only once but it was a whopper.

I had a seventieth-birthday party for Ben. We had it at Porto Bello, our house on the water in southern Maryland. I started planning it a year in advance. We had 250 guests for lunch Saturday, a seated dinner dance Saturday night, and a brunch Sunday. We bused them down from Washington, put them up at the Holiday Inn, and laid on a tennis tournament, swimming, golfing, boating, fishing, tours of historic St. Marys City, and God knows what else. We had an all-star cast made up of our dearest friends, plus an enormous tent, a band, a singer, and for the pièce de résistance we even had an air-conditioned toilet trailer complete with flower arrangements, designer soaps, and lacy sachets.

I was amazing. I was so calm throughout the entire weekend. I mean, I was *calm*. I was cool and collected. I was in a total Zen state. You have never seen anything like it. I walked around there like Napoleon before a major campaign, making the troops feel brave and lifting the morale. Nobody, including Ben, could believe it. *I* couldn't believe it. The potential for disaster on so many fronts, not the least of which had been the weather, was so great that only somebody who had had a frontal lobotomy could have been calm. Yet there I was, Miss Perfect Hostess, cool as a cucumber.

Until Sunday night.

We drove into town late Sunday afternoon, after all the luncheon guests had departed. We were both so wiped out that we collapsed into bed before nine, thinking to get the sleep of the dead. But about 3 A.M. I woke up in a cold sweat, wringing wet, soaked, and shaking so hard that the bed was jiggling. My teeth were chattering, my hands and feet were like ice cubes, and my lips were blue. It wasn't a dream. It wasn't a nightmare. It wasn't even, though at first I suspected it, some hideous virus or fever. It was pure realization. Realization of what I had attempted. Even though the celebration had been a great success, I felt like one of those pilots who go through a dogfight with the enemy, calmly shooting everyone out of the sky, and later have a major panic attack.

I know, I know, it was only a party. But I do think that, at the very least, this form of anxiety should be identified. I call it "postprandial stress syndrome."

And I don't really have any advice, except for this: get over it.

The Place

*There was a leak in the glass ceiling of the solarium and it had been
snowing on him all night long.*

I have only one rule about where to have a party. It should be someplace that's too small.

I have a large living room that I can never use for entertaining unless I am dangerously approaching P.R.F. (see earlier) territory. In this room, fifty people for cocktails looks like nobody came.

This is the key. You want your party to look like it's oversubscribed. You want it to look like every single person you invited came. You want there to be a critical mass fifteen minutes after the party begins. You want it to look like the place to be. You do not want to have pathetic little clumps of people stuck in corners whispering. You want noise, heat, electricity, excitement. You want people to be, as a friend of mine would say, "butt to butt and belly to belly."

I have a rich friend who always insists on having a small garden party every year. The problem is that she has a vast lawn that could accommodate at least five hundred people but she usually invites about thirty. She sets up two bars, one at each end of the lawn, and then essentially challenges people to find one another. The hapless guests are led by her to one of the two bars, and there they stay for the rest of the evening. Imagine thirty people on a football field. Talk about desperate little clumps of people. Even if you dared to think about mingling you'd have to find a pair of binoculars to discover who else was at the party.

On the other hand, Margaret Carlson, a columnist for *Time* magazine, who is single, has a small Georgetown house. It's actually one long narrow room downstairs, a living-dining space that flows into the kitchen. She has informal buffet suppers and cocktail parties all the time and they are among the best in town. You know when you're at Margaret's you'll have a good time because she packs 'em in and everybody there is somebody you want to talk to.

Think about this for a moment. Think about bad parties you've been to. You've gotten stuck with someone for hours and couldn't get away, right? Now if the room had been packed, all you'd have had to do is move your rear end a little, bump into someone, and then turn to apologize to the victim, and you'd be out of the boring conversation and into a new one without ever having to hurt anyone's feelings.

At a cocktail party even the most interesting person in the room is not good for more than fifteen minutes. The conversation is, by definition, more superficial at a party where the whole point is to visit with as many people as you can in a couple of hours.

I always think that having a party at your own house or apartment is nicer than having it somewhere else as long as that is the place where your guests will be most comfortable. However, there are all kinds of places to have parties that are different, original, and fun. Like having a party for someone special rather than just having a party, choosing an interesting location gives the party a focus and lends a certain energy to it.

When Quinn was six months old we had a christening for him. We were planning to have it at the National Cathedral (in one of the smaller chapels), but because two of the four godparents were Jewish, we were told we couldn't have it in an Episcopal church. Nora Ephron and Art Buchwald are Jewish, Ed Williams was a Catholic, and Ann Pincus, the only WASP, has a Jewish name. So we had it at Nora's restaurant, where we had had Larry Stern's wake.

Nora's is really like an extension of our home. It was right around the corner from our first house, near Dupont Circle, and Ben and I were original investors. There used to be a small grocery store there, a haven for drug dealers, which is why we were all so anxious to have Nora's open.

Before Quinn was born we ate many of our meals there because we were both working long hours and didn't really want to cook at eight-thirty or nine, when we got home from the paper. It started out as sort of a journalists' hangout, very informal, with exposed brick walls and beams, Windsor chairs, and old quilts instead of paintings, and has since become the best restaurant in Washington.

We took over the whole room, which wasn't very large, and set up an altar in the front. We had Father William Wendt, an Episcopal priest from an inner-city church, do the ceremony. He was more liberal than most and didn't seem to worry about the Jewish godparents. He had just come back from Israel and had brought a small bottle of water from the Sea of Galilee with which to christen Quinn. The tables and chairs were set up so that everyone could come in, get a glass of champagne, find their place cards, and take their seats. We had a harpist playing throughout the lunch. Once the christening was over, lunch was served to the guests, one of whom was the heart surgeon who had operated on Quinn. Quinn was magnificent—not a whimper—and afterward he was whisked away home for his nap. We had toasts during dessert, a lot more champagne, and it turned out to be a beautiful and very affecting day, despite or because of being held in such an unorthodox place.

Actually, entertaining in restaurants is a great and easy way to do it if you don't have a lot of time to throw a party together. Even if you do have time, you may just feel like doing something different for a change.

The thing is, don't think that because you're not having it in your own house you don't have to pay attention to the welfare of your guests. Here are a few suggestions that will make your guests feel as though you really care about them and made a special effort.

Go to the place beforehand. Decide whether you want a private room or not. (If you're expecting to have toasts, then you probably should have a private room.) If not, pick out the table you want. Make sure is isn't too big. Restaurants always want you to spread out, and then it's difficult to have a private conversation without being overheard by other patrons. If it's several long tables pushed together, be certain to have someone sitting on each end, preferably the host and hostess. It's no fun being stuck at the end of the table, feeling totally left out. Check on the air-conditioning and heating. Ask if they're going to play music, and if so, how loud. That's a nightmare as far as I'm concerned, if you care about communicating with your dinner partner. Know where you want people to sit. If you want flowers, then know what they're going to look like and how tall they are. Make sure the lights are not too bright. Finally, if you're having more than eight people you should order the meal in advance for everyone. Even with eight, I would at least order an antipasto to be shared and maybe even a dessert, a combination of several things on the menu for tasting. Then let your guests order their individual main courses if they like. The more you take care of your guests, the more special they will feel and the less they will suspect that they're being kissed off by being taken to a restaurant.

There are all kinds of unusual places to have events, places that are different even if they're not unusual. Having a barn dance in an actual barn, for instance, or a boat party or a picnic by a lake, or a clambake on the beach, for a change, can be great *as long as it is comfortable.* I emphasize this because there is nothing worse than a cute theme party where you are miserable because it is too hot, too cold, too windy, too wet, too buggy, and so forth. Too often people will plan outdoor parties and then, when the weather isn't great, they aren't prepared to change their plans and it turns out to be a disaster. I'm sure everyone can remember a time when they have been invited to some outdoor thing, only to stand forlornly in the drizzle while the hostess natters on about how it isn't so bad after all or they weren't as lucky with the weather as they had been last year.

Weather is a particular problem with tented parties, especially in winter, when the host and hostess think they can get away with it if only they have blowers. Wrong. Wrong. Wrong. I can't tell you how many times I have been to tented parties in the middle of winter where the guests have frozen their buns off.

We had a winter wedding at our house for my stepson and his wife and we invited more people than I thought the house could hold. So we had the back porch tented. The tent people assured us that the blowers would keep the porch toasty warm. Well, guess what? Not one soul set foot out on the porch. The house itself was warm and cozy, with fires blazing in all the fireplaces. The tent was freezing. When the blowers were on the noise was deafening and the hot air came right at your face. When they were off it was like the North Pole. It wasn't a catastrophe, since everyone stayed packed inside the house "belly to belly and butt to butt" and had a wonderful time, but unfortunately it cost a lot of money for nothing.

Years ago the French president Giscard d'Estaing and his wife had a black-tie dinner for President Ford and Mrs. Ford at the French embassy. It was in May, and since they had invited everyone in Washington (major P.R.F.), they had set up a tent in the backyard. However, the day before the party a record-breaking cold front moved in on Washington. Temperatures dropped down into the thirties and forties. At the last minute the embassy decided to bring in blowers to put behind the head table, and the hell with the rest of the guests. Unsuspecting, people checked their coats, including many women like me, in strapless or sleeveless dresses. There we sat, huddled together in this frigid tent, barely able to move from the cold, watching the two presidents and their wives laughing it up as the blowers blew hot air at them from behind their chairs. All I remember is grabbing on to my spoon for the soup (cold soup, of course; remember, this was May) and refusing to relinquish it to the waiter for the next course because I had warmed it up and the rest of the cutlery was too cold to touch. I ate my entire meal with the warm spoon and went home livid, certain that I would never feel the same goodwill toward the French that I had before.

When NBC correspondent Andrea Mitchell and Federal Reserve chairman Alan Greenspan got married, in April of 1997, they chose to have their wedding in the garden at one of the most beautiful country inns in America, the Inn at Little Washington. Andrea has great taste, and every detail was thought out and perfectly planned. Her dress was gorgeous, the flowers were spectacular, the menu was extraordinary. Everything worked. Except one tiny thing. Though slightly overcast, the weather was unseasonably warm, and as Andrea was setting out for the inn around eleven o'clock that morning, the inn called to ask for the final word on the tent, yes or no. Looking out and seeing sunny skies and warm temperatures, Andrea said no. The wedding was at two o'clock, only a few hours away; it was a safe call, and besides, it would look so much more beautiful without a tent hiding all the flowers.

Unfortunately, it started to rain on the way down. Andrea turned to Alan and told him she may have made the biggest mistake of their relationship. "Maybe," she joked, "we should add 'in rain or in shine' to the marriage vows."

Then the weather cleared up. But at 2 P.M. on the dot, with the guests assembled in white chairs on the terrace, all in their pastel silks and pearls, tiny wet drops began falling from the sky. The ceremony, performed by Supreme Court justice Ruth Bader Ginsburg, lasted all of seven minutes, and there was a mad dash for the door. The rain never materialized. The only thing that got wet was people's eyes, and a good time was had by all.

Andrea handled the whole thing with incredible aplomb, but

later she did laughingly concede the moral of this story: when in doubt, have a tent.

One of the funniest experiences I've had concerning the weather was at dinner in midwinter during the worst snowstorm of this century in Washington. Columnist Rowland (Rowlie) Evans and his editor wife, Kay, have a charming Federal house in Washington with a beautiful glassed-in solarium several stories high, filled with trees and light. They often entertain in the solarium when they have elegant seated dinners. On a clear night you can look up and see the moon and stars through the glass ceiling, and with only candles it is incredibly romantic. One snowy evening in February we were there for dinner with a fairly large group, and after cozy cocktails by the fireplace we were led out to the solarium, where round skirted tables had been set up. To Kay's horror, the heating was obviously not working properly and it was so cold that she went upstairs and brought down shawls and sweaters for those who were seated on the outer reaches of the terrace. I was seated between the Israeli ambassador and the governor of Maine. We shivered our way through several courses, teeth chattering. Finally, as dessert approached, the Israeli ambassador turned to me and tapped me on the arm. "Look," he whispered. I looked over and he was pointing to his shoulder. At first I thought his suit jacket was covered with dandruff and I was horrified. Then I realized it was covered with a thin layer of snow. There was a leak in the glass ceiling and it had been snowing on him all night long. Not wanting to embarrass Kay, who was on his other side, he had said nothing. Talk about being diplomatic.

I drew her attention to it and though she was initially appalled, it ended up making the evening, with everyone having a good laugh about my dinner partner, the Israeli snowman.

Being too hot is almost as bad as being too cold. Until about twenty years ago, most people in Washington didn't have centrally air-conditioned houses. I was one of them. We had only a lone air conditioner in our bedroom. It was July, when Washington is like a swamp, and I decided to have a birthday party for myself (well, I said you should have a reason for a party, and I couldn't think of a better one). I had about thirty of my friends, and within minutes after they had arrived most of them had taken off as many clothes as was decently possible. Everyone was covered with sweat within half an hour, and about an hour into the party, writer and journalist Nicholas von Hoffman came over to me, announced that it was so hot he thought he was going to faint, and with that his eyes crossed and he literally swooned right in front of me. Soon most of the guests were lying on the floor panting. (It does seem as if my guests are always on the floor. I take it as a compliment.) I found myself, like some army nurse, going around the room with glasses of water, trying to revive people. Needless to say, it was not the most successful party I've ever had. Nobody touched the food, and I don't think there was a single intelligent conversation the entire evening. There was, however, lots of gasping and moaning. The next day I called the contractor to arrange for central air-conditioning, and I've never looked back.

We moved into Georgetown several years later, and one night we had a small dinner for about eight, including Joseph Califano, former secretary of HEW, who now runs a substance-abuse think tank, and former *New York Times* executive Sydney Gruson. It was unbearably hot out, and naturally the air-conditioning wasn't working. Sweltering, we opened the window onto the street. There had just been some major bombing in the Middle East, and we were discussing it when all of a sudden we saw something come through the window and we heard a loud blast and popping noise as though a grenade had gone off. Everyone flung themselves down toward the floor, terrified, until we realized that it had only been a firecracker. Somebody walking past the house had seen us at the table and had simply thrown it at us. We quickly closed the window and got out the fans. But now, if I'm having some kind of party, I try to have the air conditioner or furnace checked beforehand to avoid having my guests either pass out from the heat or be blown to bits by a passerby.

There are all kinds of venues for parties that are fun and original. Lately some of my friends have taken to organizing surprise fiftieth- and sixtieth-birthday parties for their spouses in faraway places, like New Orleans and even Tuscany, and inviting people to join them there. Toni and Jamie Goodale organize a round-robin tennis tournament at a series of private tennis courts with an awards banquet in the evening.

Obviously, the more money you have, the more original you can get with the locations for your parties. You can rent private mansions, yachts, airplanes, islands—practically anything—if you have a lot of dough.

The thing is, you don't have to be rich to entertain well, and especially to entertain rich people. I have found that the more money people have and the more famous people are, the more they appreciate informality. They are so used to having formal seated dinners in the fanciest houses that they love to be able to relax and not have nervous hostesses hovering around trying to do things the way they think these people would want them done.

The happiest I've seen Barry Goldwater in a long time was when he arrived early for a cocktail party my mother and I were having at her apartment. We were in the kitchen making hors d'oeuvres and were running late, so we made Barry take off his jacket and tie, put on an apron, and stuff jalapeño peppers for us. The only problem was, he was having such a good time we couldn't get him out of the kitchen when the rest of the guests began to arrive.

One of my most successful impromptu dinners occurred a

night after a cocktail party, when we ended up with a few out-of-town people, including director Mike Nichols, and were deciding where to go for dinner. I suggested we go back to our house and order pizza, which we did. We sat around the kitchen table with our paper napkins, bottles of beer, and greasy pizza and told stories until very late, laughing, talking, and having a great time. Everyone kept exclaiming how nice it was to be able to just relax in the kitchen for a change.

In the end, when you think back to where you have had the most fun, it's usually in somebody's dining room or kitchen with a group of six or eight good friends, with good food, good wine, a good atmosphere, and good conversation. Which brings us to chapter six.

CHAPTER 6

The
Food

Pavarotti exclaimed that he could not eat one single thing there. A major drama ensued, with lots of emotion and hand-wringing befitting a grand opera.

My mother is one of the world's great cooks. She's a Southern cook. A Southern cook is someone who is not happy eating unless she has grease running down her elbows. Butter (or "buttah"), bacon grease, and Crisco are the staples of her kitchen. Her fried chicken is out of this world and her barbecued spareribs are the best things you've ever put in your mouth.

I've always envied my mother for the way she cooked. She was the person for whom the ad "Nuthin' says lovin' like somethin' from the oven" was made.

My mother also *loved* to cook. Nothing made her happier than an empty plate. If I had to think of one expression that would define my mother, it is "Y'all want some more?" There would be a chorus of "No, thank you's" and "It was delicious" and then she would go around the table, asking each one of us personally if we wanted anything else. Nothing would thrill her more than to have someone ask for seconds. You couldn't bear to see the look of disappointment that descended over that loving face if you said no. Food was love for her, and it went both ways. Her way of showing how much she loved us was to cook our favorite foods and make sure we were happy and well fed. But she needed us to show her how much we loved her by how much we ate. This could sometimes be a problem, particularly in later years, when I was constantly on a diet and my mother would fix the most incredibly fattening food every time we came over for dinner. I truly believe that my thighs are a result of all that love.

The thing that was so great about my mother's cooking was that it was good ole home cookin'. It wasn't fancy. She cooked the kind of food she loved to eat, the kind she grew up on. So when my father became a general and they began entertaining other generals, and ambassadors and secretaries of defense and chancellors and princes and barons and senators, my mother fed them what she liked to cook. And they loved it. Much later she would write a cookbook called *Plain Food for Fancy People*, which unfortunately never got published.

The title of her cookbook, however, shows the inspiration behind all of the parties my parents had. What it meant was (as I mentioned earlier), don't try to be something you're not. And food was a way of showing that. People like good food. Period. Wouldn't you rather have a great meat loaf and mashed potatoes than some badly done squiggly quenelles or a soggy beef Wellington with the hostess hell-bent on impressing everyone with how good a cook she is?

Remember, we're back to the beginning here. Good food is part of the guests' enjoyment. Yet a gourmet meal, no matter how good it is, is pointless if the host or hostess disappears into the kitchen for an hour while the guests are left to entertain themselves.

My mother's first dinner party was shortly after she married my father and she cooked a turkey for his commanding officer. Unfortunately she forgot to take out the little brown bag with the giblets in it and it fell out while my father was carving the turkey. Never mind, the guests loved it. All the women felt superior and all the men felt protective. Everyone secretly identified, and the party was a huge success.

My mother soon learned to be a terrific cook, and she and my father loved to entertain. Being in the army, we moved every year and a half, so there was very little time to make new friends before being transferred again. My mother and father began having a special kind of party at each new place they were stationed. Shortly after the movers arrived at the house, my parents would invite twenty or thirty people for dinner. Instead of unpacking, my mother would make a huge pot of Johnny Mazetti, a dish of noodles, cheese, tomatoes, and olives. She would have French bread, a green salad, brownies, paper plates, paper napkins, jugs of wine, and candles. People would serve themselves out of a pot in the kitchen and sit on the floor, on packing crates, or on mattresses my father had requisitioned from the quartermaster. These were always the most successful parties my parents ever had. The guests were used to seriously formal seated five-course dinners with the men in dress uniforms and decorations and the women in long dresses being served by white-gloved orderlies. Because my parents' dinners were so informal, everyone relaxed totally, had a good time, and really got to know one another in a way they never would have in other circumstances. It wasn't about cooking a gourmet dinner to impress people; it was about having a good time.

Here's my mother's recipe for Johnny Mazetti. This will serve eight people.

four pieces of bacon	one can of tomato soup
three chopped onions	two cans of tomato sauce
four pieces of celery, chopped	one can of enchilada sauce
three small green peppers, chopped	one-and-a-half pounds of grated cheddar cheese
two pounds of ground beef	one can of chopped black olives
one eight-ounce package of flat noodles	a few dashes of Tabasco sauce
two cans of chopped mushrooms	salt and pepper to taste
	six cloves of garlic

Cook the bacon. Sauté the onions, celery, and peppers in the bacon fat. Sauté the ground beef separately and pour off the liquid. Cook noodles according to the package and drain. Dump everything in a big casserole dish. Bake at 350 degrees for forty minutes covered.

Serve with pickled peaches, garlic bread, and salad.

A man's dish!

Unfortunately I did not learn cooking at the feet of the master. In my early years I had absolutely no interest in it whatsoever. My sister, Donna, inherited my mother's talent for cooking; I did not. Eating was another story. I love to eat, and love good food, and I know a lot about food. My idea of a perfect vacation is to go on an eating trip to France. As long as I don't have to cook.

This, however, was a big drawback when I got old enough to entertain, yet had no money. By then I had a job and no time either. I decided I would have to perfect one dish, so I did. Spaghetti. I have to say I made the best spaghetti sauce I have ever eaten. Better than Paul Newman's. I could do garlic bread. I could do salad, except for the dressing, which I still can't make. (I just don't understand how you can take three parts of good olive oil, one part of good vinegar, a teaspoon of Dijon mustard, salt and pepper, whip them up well, and have a dressing that is too disgusting to eat. Trust me, it can be done.)

That old spaghetti got me through a lot of potentially disastrous occasions. Since I had only one menu, I wouldn't invite people for dinner; I would invite them over for spaghetti, preempting them from saying, "Oh God, not spaghetti again." But it worked. The spaghetti was delicious, and we always had plenty of wine and some gooey chocolate dessert (which I bought).

I'm not giving you my recipe for spaghetti. It's all I've got.

In those days, when nobody had any money, we often would have dinner parties where everyone brought something. I brought my spaghetti. Sometimes, if everyone was sick of it, I'd bring a store-bought dessert. This was a good idea for entertaining and still is when everyone wants to get together but nobody has time to cook or wants to spend a lot on a caterer or gourmet carryout.

My only problem with the covered-dish event is that if it's at my house, I don't have control. Susie may say she's going to bring corn pudding, then change her mind at the last minute and bring sushi, and it throws off the whole dinner scheme. Holidays are the only time I do this, and since people have their own family customs and traditions, it's always nice to blend in other kinds of foods. I just cook what I want and then eat what I want of the other dishes.

One of the reasons I didn't learn to cook until quite late is that I lived with Warren Hoge, who loved to cook and was terrific at it. In fact, when we broke up the only thing we fought about was the fish poacher. He got it. This was only fair, since I had never poached a fish in my life.

One of the best parties I've ever had was a dinner in honor of Fleur Cowles, author, painter, socialite, and an old friend of my parents, who was visiting from London. My parents had planned to have a dinner for her but my father had to go out of town unexpectedly on business and they asked me to have it instead. Among the guests were Ambassador David Bruce and his wife, Evangeline. Bruce had been ambassador to England and France and his wife had been one of the great hostesses of our time. They lived in a beautiful house in Georgetown and entertained constantly. I invited a number of famous and successful journalists, columnists, television personalities, and diplomats. I was in my late twenties at the time, single, a beginning reporter for the *Washington Post,* and I lived in a tiny apartment in the Dupont Circle area, the hippie part of town in those days.

Naturally it was a buffet supper, since I had no dining room. I decided to serve my mother's old standby, Johnny Mazetti, with garlic bread and salad, and brownies for dessert. Mother had loaned me her electric casserole cooker. I fixed the casserole, put it in the electric cooker, made the salad and the bread, put out the flowers and candles, made sure I had plenty of booze (thank God), and got dressed, feeling pretty secure that we were going to have a good time.

Two things my mother had taught me were: never cook something for a party you hadn't tried to cook before, and always prepare as much as you can beforehand so you'll have time to spend with your guests and you won't be a total wreck. I wasn't nervous at all. My parents never were, and their parties always turned out wonderfully well.

Everyone arrived around 8 P.M. It was a good group and people were mixing and mingling and really enjoying themselves. I went to get the food ready around 9 P.M., only to find it stone cold. I called a friend into the kitchen for consultation, we turned up the heat on the cooker, and I poured everyone more drinks. At nine-thirty and then again at ten I checked, only to find the food still cold. Finally one of the men came into the kitchen, looked at the machine, and discovered to my amazement that I had forgotten to plug it in. By this time people were on their fourth or fifth drink. At eleven, dinner was served. One well-known TV anchorman was close to passing out, and Ambassador Bruce, then near eighty, was in my bedroom, lying on the bed, with the door open, trying to make out with Barbara Howar. I don't think anyone ever actually ate the Johnny Mazetti.

Until she died, a year ago, every time I saw Evangeline Bruce she would tell me that that party was the best party she had ever been to.

So much for food.

You can see why, after that, I was never that motivated to learn how to cook.

Shortly after Ben and I got together we moved into a one-bedroom apartment in the Watergate. Unfortunately, I had neglected to tell him I couldn't boil water. One night when he came home from the *Post* (I was working at home writing a book) he announced that his old friend Eppie Lederer, aka Ann Landers, was coming to town and he had asked her to dinner the next night.

"Can't we take her out to dinner?" I begged.

"Oh, no," he said, "she's dying to see our apartment and I think it would be nicer and more relaxing just to eat here."

I protested feebly for a while, to no avail.

The next morning, panicked, I called a friend who was a good cook. She told me to go to the store, get a certain brand of frozen stuffed bell peppers, take them out of the package, put them in a nice casserole dish, cook them, and ladle sour cream all over them.

"They're delicious," she said, "and Eppie will never know. Just say it's an old family recipe."

I did what she said. Eppie arrived, we had cocktails, and then, with trepidation, I served dinner.

Ben had seconds and beamed all the way through. His little helpmate had surprisingly turned out to be a brilliant cook. Eppie had at least seconds, maybe thirds. She raved and raved and couldn't stop talking about the peppers. The best thing she had ever put in her mouth. I told her it was an old family recipe. "My mother's a great cook," I said, not lying about that anyway. She wanted the recipe. My heart sank.

"I'll send it to you," I promised, hoping she would forget.

No such luck. She called several times for the recipe and I could tell she was getting annoyed that I wasn't sending it. I was desperate. What should I do? I confessed to Ben. I could see he was deeply disappointed in me.

"Just tell the truth," said Mr. Watergate sternly. Finally, I bit the bullet and wrote Eppie a *Dear Ann Landers* letter explaining what I had done and asking for advice. Happily she thought it was very funny and was extremely gracious about the whole thing.

The lesson here is, if you can't cook, go out and buy some frozen stuffed bell peppers, put them in a nice casserole dish, ladle them with sour cream, and say it's an old family recipe.

Several years later, however, I had had a stint on TV as the anchorwoman for the *CBS Morning News*, and with the money I earned, I bought myself a small house in the Dupont Circle area a few blocks from where my bachelorette apartment had been. Ben and I moved out of our Watergate apartment and into my new house.

It was a time when everybody was doing competitive cooking. I caught the bug, and with my mother's help I began to actually enjoy it. I started reading cookbooks instead of novels at night, getting a taste of the world of Julia Child and Marcella Hazan.

One evening we had Nora Ephron and Carl Bernstein over for dinner and I decided I was going to go for the gold and make my own pasta for the first time (breaking my mother's ironclad rule). I had gotten a pasta machine for Christmas and, with my newfound confidence, just knew I could pull it off. Sadly, it was spinach pasta I had chosen to make, not a felicitous choice. When Nora and Carl arrived I was standing in the kitchen frantically grinding out these disgusting slimy green squiggles that resembled nothing remotely like pasta as we know it.

I was humiliated but valiant, and I was also prepared, having laid on a supply of store-bought fettuccine in case the worst happened.

Well, guess what? I made a great Alfredo sauce with shrimp. And with crusty garlic bread and salad, and some delicious store-bought lemon tart for dessert, the dinner was great.

The pasta dinner was shortly before the night that Nora and Carl broke up. That happened at another dinner at our house, a lobster dinner several months later. Unbeknownst to us, Nora had recently learned that Carl was having an affair with the wife of the British ambassador (the aforementioned Margaret Jay), also the daughter of the prime minister. As we began innocently talking about how it was impossible not to know if your spouse was having an affair, Nora stood up, asked for a bottle of red wine (we were drinking white), and poured it over Carl's head. (Happily, the kitchen floor was tiled.)

Later, in her best-selling 1983 novel and movie, *Heartburn*, she changed the wine pouring to a pie in the face. But all in all it was a memorable evening, and the food, though good, was the least of it.

Several years later I was having a seated dinner for twelve. By this time we had moved to Georgetown, had a much grander house, and I kept thinking I had to have fancy parties. This one night I had an author friend from New York, and several political types and journalists he wanted to meet. I had arranged to have dinner catered. The menu was planned, the flowers arranged, the candles set out, the napkins and tablecloth pressed. The caterers were supposed to show up an hour before the party. When they didn't arrive I began calling. There was no answer. (It turned out there was a mixup on the date.) Finally, frantic, I asked the baby-sitter to go out to Popeye's for food. She came back with cartons of fried chicken, red beans and rice, corn bread, biscuits, collard greens—the works. I quickly put the food out on the buffet on my best china with my best silver. I can't tell you how they raved over the food. Everyone went back for seconds and the next day two people called for the name of the caterer. Plus, we had a lot of fun. The food was informal, and since everyone was eating the chicken with their fingers, I made the men take off their coats and ties, which relaxed people even more. It was a great evening and I learned an important lesson about food, too. It doesn't matter what it is or who makes it. It only has to be good.

What was special about my mother's cooking and my mother's attitude toward feeding either her family or her guests was that it wasn't about her. It was about pleasing other people. Certainly she had an ego—she was only human—and she adored it when people complimented her on her food. But what really motivated her was making other people happy.

A friend of mine visited my mother at the hospital several

years ago after she had had a series of debilitating strokes. (These ultimately rendered her not only unable to cook but even to eat anything that wasn't pureed.) My mother was describing how to make clam chowder, and my friend said that her description of how to make it was so loving in the details and in the obvious desire to please her guests that it was very touching.

My mother's attitude is so different from that of so many "cooks," who entertain but think the whole event is about them and their food. The guests are mere props at their table, supporting actors in the play, while the cook gets the starring role. We are expected to exclaim and applaud at every course, and a standing ovation is expected at the end—even if the food isn't great. Often these people, male or female, will overreach, cooking something they've never cooked before or something that is much too complicated for a private dinner party. No matter. Just eat and vow never to be that way yourself.

I am not talking here about world-famous chefs. If you get asked to Julia Child's for dinner it will certainly be about the food —although, she is such a delightful person that I'm sure she would feel the evening was a failure if people came only to eat and not to enjoy the company.

I have plenty of friends who are perfectly good cooks and serve wonderful food but don't expect you to worship their offering and discuss it interminably. Nora Ephron is a fabulous and seemingly effortless cook, and with the help of her brilliant sous-chef and husband, writer Nick Pileggi, she always has great parties. The food is the best, but it's never just about the food. Ken Auletta makes the best Italian food I have ever eaten, and with the expert assistance of superagent Binky Urban, his wife, their parties are warm, fun, and relaxed, and we all eat ourselves into oblivion.

They understand the point is to have a good time. The food, important as it is, is secondary.

When I was cooking, during that small window between the time I bought my house and the time I got pregnant, I actually enjoyed it, and I could serve an entire dinner, which I had prepared earlier, for thirty-five or forty guests after a day at the office. I was always happy when they complimented me on the food. But I was always happier if they had a good time. If they raved about the food and filed out of there at 10 P.M., then I would know the party was a bomb, and it didn't matter to me that they loved what they ate.

I wish I were a good enough cook and had the time to cook all the food for my parties. But I don't, and I've gotten over it. The one thing I really care about is that the food taste and look as if I might have cooked it. This is not meant to deceive, it's only to please the guest. There is nothing like a home-cooked meal. If I have a party catered, the first thing I always tell the caterers is that I want it to appear homemade. And I almost always have a tasting first before a big party. When I had that seventieth-birthday party for Ben we had a tasting, and though everything tasted fine, it wasn't great. After several hours of our sending things back and experimenting, they had perfected the menu and it was wonderful.

Just an aside here. As it is important to have a tasting before a big event, so also it is important to know your caterer's reputation and make sure that they send only people they know well to do the serving. I had a large seated dinner some years back and the caterer I had used forever had an unusual number of events that night. They were low on staff and hired two waiters they had never used to send to my party, along with several others who had been to the house before. Unfortunately the two waiters got totally stoned, acted really weird during the dinner, and after dinner went into the laundry room, grabbed several of my bras and panty hose from the dryer, and hung them from the chandelier.

My advice here is: if the caterer needs to use people they don't know, get them to send them to somebody else's party.

There is nothing I hate worse than an overly catered meal. A designer meal, I think it's called. I don't want a designer meal when I go to somebody's house. I'll get that in a restaurant. I want to feel warm and cozy and loved when I go out, and I want my guests to feel the same way. I do not want to eat Burmese crayfish with kiwi and quinoa in a raspberry balsamic dressing with sun-dried tomatoes when I go to a friend's house for dinner. Or ever, for that matter.

At our last New Year's Eve party I served choucroute (sauer-kraut with ham and sausages) and mashed potatoes. One man came up to me and kissed me on the cheek, thanking me for the mashed potatoes. You would have thought I had served him a private cache of the shah's golden caviar.

On the other hand, it's nice to be a little inventive if you're having guests over, and not make it look like they would have gotten the same fare if they had dropped by the night before. You want them to think you've made a special effort for them.

Obviously there are different kinds of food for different kinds of parties. If you're having a seated dinner you will have different food than you would if you were having a cocktail buffet.

These days everybody seems to be dieting, and more and more people are vegetarians. This is tricky for the host or hostess. Here's what I do. I serve a sinfully rich dinner but with a lot of vegetables. This is on the theory that people are going out to dinner, not to a health spa, but that if they want to diet they can stick to the beans and carrots. I also make sure that there are no courses that are only meat.

Generally people will let the hostess know if they have special dietary problems or they'll eat beforehand and say nothing. But you always have to be prepared for emergencies.

My neighbor Yolande Fox, the former Miss America, from Alabama, had a party several years ago for the great Italian tenor Luciano Pavarotti. Everyone was excited about meeting him, but none as excited as her caterer, who actually created a new and special pasta sauce for him, Sauce Pavarotti, of which she was especially proud.

The party got off to a good start when, to our delight, Pavarotti went over to the piano and gave a singing lesson to Yolande's daughter Dolly.

The situation deteriorated when Yolande summoned everyone into the dining room, where she had a sumptuous buffet laid out. Pavarotti took one look at the table and exclaimed that he was on a special diet and could not eat one single thing there. A major drama ensued, with lots of emotion and hand-wringing befitting a grand opera. Yolande had nothing else in the house, not even a piece of lettuce. Finally it was determined that Pavarotti could eat lobster, so she had to send out for the lobster to a specialty store that was open late and the crisis was solved. But there was hostess's blood all over the floor, nonetheless.

An official Washington dinner party until recently used to be the ultimate nightmare in terms of amount of food and length of time you spent at the table.

I remember the days when I first started covering parties for the *Washington Post* "Style" section. The embassy parties were absolute killers. They usually had five courses, and sometimes six, and wine with each course. They would start with a terrapin soup with sherry, then a fish course with white wine, then a meat course with a red wine, then a salad-and-cheese course with the same red wine, and finally a dessert course with dessert wine or champagne. Often there would be a sorbet to freshen the palate between the fish and the meat course, and then there would be liqueurs served after dinner. You can imagine how deadly this could be if you had unfortunate dinner partners, not to mention how filling.

Today almost nobody serves more than three courses. On a "school night," long, drawn-out dinners with too much food and wine only make the guests surly and hostile. There are, as always, exceptions. When the rare host or hostess has a great private chef whose food is spectacular, such dinners are always a treat, and people know what they're getting before they come. If it's a special occasion like an anniversary or a birthday, particularly if it's on a weekend and people don't have to work the next day, then it's acceptable to have more food. If it's a small dinner party and you can have group conversation, that's OK too. But if you're going to serve more than three courses, you had better make sure your guests are all seated next to somebody they like a lot, because there is nothing more depressing than to get stuck with a dog of a dinner partner for an interminable meal. I generally don't serve more than three courses just because I can't eat that much and I don't want people to feel stuck. I'm not asking them to spend the night, only to have dinner.

If you're having a buffet supper, whether it's seated or not, you can have several different dishes for the guests to choose from, and they can get up and down from the table, or the sofa, mixing and mingling as they go.

If it's not seated, I try never to have anything that requires heavy-duty cutting. Curry or something like that, which you can eat with a fork alone, is always a good bet. I can't tell you how many times I've tried to cut something on a plate in my lap and sent the plate, the food, or both halfway across the room.

The opposite, of course, of too much food is too little food. This is the personal nightmare of any Southern host or hostess. (My husband is a Yankee and doesn't appreciate it when I say this, but you could starve to death at a Yankee's house and nobody would notice.) My parents used to have Yankee friends, very rich and very fancy, who entertained constantly. They often had buffet suppers, and when they did it was a family joke that you raced to the line first or you wouldn't get to eat because they always ran out of food.

When Evangeline and David Bruce came back to Washington after his ambassadorial postings, and particularly after he died, she almost completely gave up having dinner parties and took to having Sunday brunches. These were very peculiar affairs. Instead of serving lunch, she would have hors d'oeuvres passed. These hors d'oeuvres, usually some kind of seafood or tiny deviled quail's eggs, would be hidden in large trays full of seaweed, so they were hard to find and difficult to distinguish. You would be asked for lunch or brunch at noon. Then you would stand out on the terrace if the weather was warm, or inside if not, trying to balance a drink and a handbag while shaking hands and trying to maneuver a large, unwieldy, sometimes dripping hors d'oeuvre to your mouth and back, making it look graceful. Another Washington hostess, Joan Braden, once remarked of these lunches, "I find it impossible to eat and kiss at the same time."

If you'd been there before, you knew the drill and you would eat before you went. The initiates would delight in watching newcomers stand around looking at their watches, waiting to be told lunch was served, declining the hors d'oeuvres for fear of spoiling their appetites.

My husband finally rebelled and refused to go anymore, citing the seaweed as the offensive factor. This was after the Princess Margaret lunch. Evangeline had a lunch in honor of Princess Margaret, at which everyone dutifully appeared. We arrived at noon, as did the guest of honor, who was escorted by an old friend of mine from New York, the executive vice president of the Metropolitan Museum of Art, Ashton Hawkins. We stood around for an hour or so, those of us in the know, scarfing up the baby shrimps and mussels as fast as we could. The princess was drinking something brown that appeared to be bourbon in a large glass, which was constantly being refilled by a waiter. As two o'clock rolled around, I found Ashton in the corner. It was hot and we were all beginning to perspire. "When do you think lunch will be served?" he asked. "I'm starving and so is she." "Starving" is not exactly the word I would have used to describe the princess.

I had to break the bad news to him that lunch, in fact, had been served. "Oh God" was all he could say. He looked desperately in the direction of Princess Margaret, who was accepting another drink and who was at that moment taking my husband by the arm and removing him to a sofa in the far corner of the room, where they sat for nearly another hour alone.

"That's it," said Ben on the way home. "No more stand-up" —"falling down" might have been a more appropriate expression—"seaweed lunches for me."

Evangeline once gave an interview explaining the rationale behind the lunches. She said that it was just too hard trying to do seated lunches or dinners in Washington because it was too difficult to get an equal number of men and women, and besides, people just didn't show up, and then you had to rearrange the table at the last minute, and she was sick of it. That was understandable, but still, it just didn't work. She was entertaining for her own convenience rather than for the comfort and pleasure of her guests.

Which brings us back to hors d'oeuvres. Big, fat, greasy, lumpy things that require three or four bites, smear your lipstick, and get food caught in your teeth are the worst. I'm a fanatic about small, single-bite–sized hors d'oeuvres you can pop in your mouth and swallow in one gulp, then continue on with the conversation without having to juggle something in your hand along with your drink and everything else. If you want to serve large, unwieldy hors d'oeuvres, then put them on the buffet and have little plates so people can choose to deal with them if they're really hungry or if they don't mind the hassle. Also, try to skip really fishy-smelling hors d'oeuvres or big hunks of cheese, which don't do much for people's breath. My all-time most hated hors d'oeuvre is the cherry tomato stuffed with crabmeat. They're too big for one bite, they squirt and drip, they leave your breath smelling fishy, and they get stuck in your teeth. My number-one favorite is the cheese straw, or cheese stick. They are delicious, easy to eat, and not too filling. These may seem small and unimportant details, but the whole purpose of the exercise is to make sure your guests are happy. Nobody's happy if they've got someone talking at them at close range who's just eaten a big mouthful of seafood, and if you're the one talking, you're not going to be happy fearing you might be offending people.

I also never serve a lot of heavy hors d'oeuvres before a dinner party. People fill up on them and it ruins their appetite, and they don't enjoy the meal. If you're going to the time, effort, and expense of having a dinner party, don't load up your guests with a lot of food beforehand. It defeats the purpose, and nobody expects it anyway.

The prevailing notion these days is that it's not original or chic to have a buffet table with a ham at one end and a turkey at the other with biscuits. I'm always hearing derisive comments about hostesses who don't have any more imagination than to serve a ham or a turkey. I think that's ridiculous. Everyone loves ham and everyone loves turkey. Nothing thrills me more than when I see a buffet table laid out with a great country ham and a crisp roasted turkey and homemade biscuits with lots of mustards and mayonnaise and chutneys. It's real food, for God's sake. Again, the whole point is to please your guests. Let the complainers in the corner titter about lack of originality while the rest of your happy guests hunker down to great food and accept your next invitation with alacrity.

Speaking of ham, one thing my mother taught me about having successful parties was that a smart hostess always serves either ham or bacon. The reason for this is that the ham and bacon are salty and they will make people thirsty and they will drink more. If they drink more, they'll have a better time and the party will be a success. To this day, even though getting my guests tight is not a priority, I always try to serve either ham or crispy bacon for hors d'oeuvres, if for no other reason than good luck. They're almost like talismans to me in this age of low cholesterol.

While we're on the subject, the final word on food: just re-member, no matter how bad the food is or what disaster befalls you in the kitchen, when all else fails, make sure you have plenty of booze on hand, and the party won't be a total bomb.

CHAPTER 7

The
Booze

*I hereby give all hosts and hostesses permission to refuse to serve
red wine at P.R.F.'s.*

When talking about party giving I include food and wine in the same category. I'm sure that to a wine expert this would be a travesty, but so be it. In fact, I include all alcoholic beverages in one category.

First of all, I think it is almost impossible to have a hugely successful party without having some alcoholic beverages. When I say that, I mean a party in the evening. I am not counting church socials, lunches, or children's birthday parties. Even so, without any alcohol at all, you're not going to have a rollicking good time. Alcohol relaxes people and loosens their inhibitions. Not only that, but good wine is delicious. The serving of alcohol also lends the party a more festive atmosphere, and it distinguishes the party from a purely work- or duty-oriented event. I do not mean that your guests have to be drunk in order for the party to be successful, nor do I mean that a person cannot have a good time without drinking. I simply mean that the party as a whole ends up being more fun if people are drinking booze. Period.

These days there is more awareness of the dangers of drunk driving. I certainly don't want my friends to get blotto. In fact, nothing ruins a party faster than a sloppy drunk. But you hardly ever see that happening anymore, anyway. Most of my friends are so aware of the new responsibilities that usually couples will designate one or the other to drive. I find that if people come knowing they're going to drink they will come in a cab or come with friends or even hire a car for the evening. If I see somebody who really has had too much to drink I'll tell that person not to drive and offer to call a cab. That hasn't happened often but I have done it occasionally. And nobody was offended or hurt by it either. I don't want it on my conscience that a guest of mine got killed or injured, or killed or injured someone else.

For cocktail parties I always have wine and beer as well as hard liquor for mixed drinks. I don't drink hard liquor but I know a lot of people who get very surly when they arrive at a cocktail party and find only wine and beer. There does seem to be something a little cheap about just wine and beer. My feeling is that if you can afford the party at all you can spring for a bottle of gin and a bottle of scotch.

For cocktail parties I think it is dumb to serve a really spectacular wine. I always choose a good, midpriced, very dry white wine that will appeal to everyone's palate. For one thing, many people these days ask for spritzers, or white wine and soda, and I always ask for a lot of ice in mine if I'm the designated driver or if I know it will be a while before dinner.

Here's the one thing I can think of that I do or ever have done that puts my convenience over the pleasure of my guests. If I'm having a P.R.F. I refuse to serve red wine. I know this is mean and ungracious, but I have had too many catastrophes to ever want to do it again. People spill; they just do. People jostle one another, they embrace one another, they gesticulate (remember, it's always better to have a too-crowded room), they sit on the floor, and they knock glasses of red wine out of other people's hands and onto my white damask sofa, and it makes me crazy. Yes, I know, you can pour soda water over it and pour salt over it, but it never looks the same, and I've actually had to have furniture re-covered at great expense because of spilled red wine. Not to mention white rugs.

I rationalize this rule by telling myself that the guest feels much worse having ruined a beautiful piece of furniture than he or she would by having to drink a glass of white wine instead of red. So I hereby give all hosts and hostesses permission to refuse to serve red wine at P.R.F.'s.

I love good wine, but I am not a wine snob. I used to be, but it was too much trouble, and finally too boring. I used to know all the vineyards and all the good years and bad years, and I was able to rattle them off, and then I grew up and realized how incredibly tedious wine snobs are, and I've lived happily ever after. Drinking fairly well, thank you very much. I do have a few friends who really do know their wines and care a great deal about them, and I'm very impressed and appreciative of their knowledge. They are not phonies. If you really know and care about wines and even have your own cellar, serve it to your guests' delight. But don't go on about it all night the way some cooks go on about their food. The only thing worse than a wine snob is a wine bore. And never try to fake knowledge about wine. There is always someone who will know more than you do, and you will inevitably end up looking like an ass. I know. I've been there.

My tastes in wine have changed a great deal over the years. I also have enough confidence in myself that I can serve what I want and what I like, and if somebody thinks that's not the best wine, I don't give a damn. I want to drink what I want to drink, and if it's not "a good year," so be it. I now like only very dry white wines, like the Italian ones, specifically Pinot Grigio. Most other whites, like a Montrachet that I used to love, just taste too fruity or heavy to me now. I feel the same way about most reds. Though I love the taste of a really good burgundy, like a Pommard, they kill me. They keep me awake at night and leave me with terrible headaches in the morning. So I find I go for a very light Beaujolais instead. Years ago rosé was all the rage, and I remember loving it. Then it went out of fashion. Now it's back in again, or so I'm told, which doesn't matter to me except that I've been served it recently and I find it very pleasant and easy to drink. It also solves the problem of having to choose between red or white for meat or fish. You can get away with serving a good rosé with both red and white meat. The red-or-white problem is sometimes overdone but it's there for a reason. I don't find a light white wine as satisfying with a great big thick steak as I do a red wine. And I don't really like a heavy red wine with a fillet of sole. There are exceptions, but it makes more sense just to stick with the rule—white wine for white meat and red wine for red meat—and that way you'll be sure not to make a mistake.

If you're having a dinner party I think it is important to make sure you have a decent wine to serve your guests. You never have to impress anyone, particularly if you don't know your wines. Just skip the jug wines for parties. If you feel insecure about your choice of wines, ask your liquor store dealer, or if you're having the party catered, ask the caterer to help you choose something. That's what I do. I'll ask the liquor store dealer what he has that's really good in a given price range, and I'll almost always get a good choice. Just be sure to try a bottle several days before the party to make sure you like it. If your guests don't like it, let's hope they will have the decency to stay silent. This is assuming, of course, that you don't serve rotgut. But frankly I have no patience with wine snobs. Don't forget, however, that if you have a nice drinkable wine, yet one that probably wouldn't bring much at a Sotheby's auction, it will only make your guests feel superior. This is good because as a hostess your goal is always to make your guests happy.

If I'm having a seated dinner with several courses I usually will have a white wine with the first course and a red wine with the second course if it's some kind of meat. If not, I'll stick with white all the way through. Most people will drink white, but there are a lot of people who just can't tolerate red wine. It literally makes them sick. So you should always have white on hand no matter what you're serving. If I'm having a seated buffet supper, I will offer both all the way through the meal. I also always have plenty of beer. I've noticed more and more people are drinking it and even asking if they can carry it in to dinner with them. It's lighter, you don't get as high on it, and you don't have a hangover if you have to work the next day. If people want to drink beer with their meal, that's fine with me. The whole point is to please your guests. They can drink Gatorade for all I care as long as it makes them happy.

If the party is celebrating something or someone, it's nice to have champagne at dessert. I don't do it ordinarily and it does get expensive, but for special birthdays, anniversaries, promotions, and things like that it is a very gracious way to congratulate someone and it lends a festive atmosphere to the party. It's also nice to have for toasts. If it's a really special party I might actually serve champagne all the way through the meal, but that would usually be for something very small and very unusual. I always have champagne for Christmas dinner, but that's simply because I am so near death from exhaustion by the time we sit down that I don't think I could make it without champagne. And I always have champagne on New Year's Eve.

Forget after-dinner liqueurs. Nobody needs them, and these days it just seems really pretentious for a tray with little glasses to appear after dinner when everyone is ready to go home. There are exceptions. If somebody has given you a great bottle of brandy for Christmas or you've picked up an incredible bottle of Poire on your last trip to France, by all means tell your guests and offer it as a special treat. But make it mean something. Don't do it just to show off. If you and your friends all serve after-dinner liqueurs and everyone expects it and enjoys it, then that's fine. It's just that if you are unsure whether or not to do it, don't. When in doubt, leave it out.

People are drinking less these days for all the reasons I've mentioned and often will switch to water in the middle of the meal. I normally don't serve water with the meal but I probably should. I've noticed that recently at a lot of dinners I've been happy to have water in front of me, especially if things dragged on.

I'm very bad about coffee after dinner. I probably should serve it but most of the time I don't, even though, if I have a party catered, I always end up having a fight with the caterer about it. Here's my reasoning: it kills the party. If everyone is drinking wine and laughing and carrying on and suddenly they are presented with coffee, the message is clear: "The party's over. It's time to call it a day," as the old song goes. What happens is they take the coffee, they put down their wine, they drink their coffee, and then they all get up and leave. Most of them don't even want the coffee, but they take it anyway. If it's served after they've left the table, they put it on tables or on the floor and then trip over it. At dinners it should always be decaffeinated if you serve it at all, but even that has some caffeine, and it keeps you awake anyway.

Sometimes caterers serve caffeinated coffee by mistake. If it's served at all at dinner parties I would rather it be served in small cups or demitasse rather than large cups, which seem so unappetizing after a big meal and a lot of wine. The question is then whether to serve it at the table or after the guests have left the table. I'm of two minds about this. If you serve it at the table it sort of flows with the dessert and the rest of the meal. However, if you have a dog of a dinner partner, seeing the coffee brought in just as you thought you might be about to escape is almost enough to send you over the edge.

On the other hand, if the dinner is over, you've left the table, and then coffee is served, it means you have to stay just when you thought you were going to make an early night of it. In Washington a lot of dinners are official and people are semiworking, so they are often grateful for a little coffee at the end of the meal to keep them awake on the drive home. But I don't have official parties. I have parties only for fun. And I always think that coffee spoils the fun. So my advice is, bag the coffee.

A final word on booze. Nothing makes me crazier than to go to a dinner party and sit having a conversation with an empty glass in front of me. Nothing kills a party faster, either, than to look around the table and see people reaching for empty glasses. I always have more chilled wine than I need (warm white wine is like drinking bathwater). If I'm doing it myself I'll keep a couple of ice buckets nearby with the chilled wine, which I open, so I don't have to keep jumping up and down to get it. Sometimes I'll keep a tiny crystal ice bucket on the table to pass around if the wine starts getting warm. And it's a nice idea to have wine coasters on the table for the red wine so guests can just help themselves. If I have help the one thing I tell them is to make sure there is never an empty glass on the table. Particularly if I have to make a toast, I want to make sure my guests are forgiving before I get up to make a fool out of myself.

I think this was taken to the extreme a while ago when I was planning a toast and I was quite nervous about it. The party was catered and I explained to the waiters that I wanted the drinks stiff and the wineglasses filled to the brim all the way through dinner. That was my only chance of pulling it off. The day after the party a friend called to thank me and admit that he was feeling slightly hungover. At some point I mentioned how nervous I had been about the toast.

"Oh," he said, "you gave a toast?"

CHAPTER 8

The *Setting*

*"Five thousand dollars," he says threateningly, sticking out his right
hand, "that there are other people in turtlenecks."*

We've already talked about where to have a party and what to serve. Now let's talk about how to make it as attractive and comfortable as possible for your guests. Since I'm basically a Southerner I am always cold, so I'm a fanatic about room temperature. I hate being too cold. The perfect temperature in a room is around seventy-two degrees. That's comfortable for most people. Often if you're having a party, particularly if it's large, it requires adjusting the temperature once or even several times during an evening. I don't understand the mentality behind keeping a room cold when guests arrive because you know it's going to warm up later. What does that say to your guests? Sorry, you'll just have to freeze your behind off until everyone else gets here . . .

As an army brat, one of the things I learned early on is that first impressions are extremely important. If I started out in a class making straight A's my first marking period, the teacher identified me as an A student. Even if I didn't do so well later, I was given the benefit of the doubt.

Parties are much like that. If you walk in and everything looks and feels great, your first impression is that it's going to be a good party. Even if things fall apart as the evening goes on, you have a positive view of the situation and it will take a lot to turn that around.

The room should feel good. It shouldn't be too cold or too hot, but too cold is worse because it's not cozy. This applies in summer too, when I've often spent more miserable evenings in people's houses because of the air-conditioning than I have because of cold in the winter. In winter I will often turn the heat down as the party gets going, everyone arrives, and it gets hotter, then turn it back up as things begin to thin out. If I have a group that I feel is a little stiff, I'll deliberately turn up the heat or down the air conditioner, depending on the season, just before we sit down for dinner. Then I'll announce to the men they should take off their jackets if they're too warm. Gratefully they take off their jackets and roll up their sleeves. Nothing loosens up an uptight crowd more than having the men feel like they're breaking the rules a little bit. Then I'll quietly go adjust the temperature so that people are genuinely comfortable.

Fireplaces make a big difference. I hate to see an empty, dead fireplace in the winter or in cold weather. Even though I don't subscribe to Richard Nixon's habit of turning up the air-conditioning in summer so he could light the fire, I'm sympathetic with the longing for a hearth. A roaring fire says warmth and hospitality and safety and protection. There's an atavistic quality to it, a visceral draw toward the hearth that is irresistible. It's the most welcoming thing in a house. I know people think it's too much trouble, but now they even have gas fires and logs you can buy in the drugstore, which burn for three or four hours at a time. So it's not like you have to go out and chop down a tree yourself in order to have a fire for your guests. I look at an empty fireplace in winter and think the hosts didn't want to bother, and it doesn't make me feel very special.

Lighting is crucial. Lighting sets the mood. Bad lighting can literally ruin a party. How much fun can you have when you feel as if you're about to be interrogated by the police, with a light shining in your face? How much fun can you have if you know the person you are talking to can see every pore in your face?

Everyone likes to look good. Why do movie stars have the camera lens covered with gauze or Vaseline? Think of lighting a party the way you would light a set for a movie and think of your guests as the stars. Not only does it make people feel good to think they look great, but it also makes them feel good to be in a room full of great-looking people. This can't happen with a lot of high wattage.

Evangeline Bruce (yes, the Evangeline of the seaweed) once commented to me at a dinner at the British embassy that somebody had to tell the ambassador's wife about the lights. They were far too bright, she said, and flattered no one. In fact, they made people look old. It is true that in the great hall of the embassy, the overhead chandeliers are often so brightly lit that it looks as if they're set up for night baseball.

Bright lights make people look older and less attractive. Soft lights are romantic, sexy, and they make people look younger and more beautiful. It's that simple. I always use pink lightbulbs for parties. They give off a soft, welcoming glow and just make everything look better. I also have a rose-colored living room, and at night the light bounces off the walls. As one of my male guests once remarked to me, it gives everyone a sort of "postcoital flush." That does tend to perk things up.

All lights should be on dimmers, particularly the kitchen lights. Half the time at parties, especially informal ones, everyone ends up in the kitchen, and a lot of people have no lamps in their kitchens. (I have three, but I'm a lighting nut.) *When in doubt, dim* is my feeling. Sometimes caterers don't like it much when they're tripping over one another and trying to feel their way around in the gloaming, but you've got to have priorities.

You can't have too many candles. Your house should look like high mass on Christmas Eve or Barbra Streisand's bathtub in *A Star Is Born*. I use lots of candles everywhere—in the entrance hall, on the mantels, on side tables and sideboards, even in the chandeliers. And I use a lot of votive candles because they're small and you can tuck them away in lots of places.

I prefer white candles to colored ones simply because I think they're prettier and there's something pure, elegant, and celebratory about white candles. This is not some sort of edict, such as "One never uses anything but white." This is just my preference. One of the all-time great decorators, Rose Cumming, was famous for her black candles and was hailed as being terribly chic because of them. I don't like black candles. I find them scary. There's something Charles Addamsy about them. The message is: someone's going to be sacrificed tonight and it could be the guests. I don't mind red and green candles at Christmas, and scented candles are usually different colors. But in general I think white candles are nicer.

I will give you this warning about candles, though. They can be dangerous, and you certainly don't want to immolate your guests. So if you have them on side tables, make sure the tables are tall enough and out of the flow enough so that people's clothes don't catch on fire.

This actually happened one night at a party I was covering for the *Post* years ago. Lorraine Cooper, one of Washington's preeminent hostesses and wife of Kentucky senator John Sherman Cooper, was having a cocktail party at their beautiful house in Georgetown. Mrs. Cooper's living room was, as usual, candlelit, and she had one low side table next to a chair with an antique sterling silver candlestick and a burning candle in it. At one point a friend of Mrs. Cooper, dressed in a long red flowing chiffon evening dress, walked over to her hostess to say good night. Just as she was reaching over to kiss her good-bye the kimono sleeve of her dress caught the flame and lit up like a torch. Both ladies shrieked at the top of their lungs, and as I recall, one of the waiters quickly took off his jacket and smothered the fire before the poor woman was roasted. Happily, nobody was hurt and the incident gave everyone "a little frisson," as one of the guests remarked, which actually livened up what could have been a rather dull evening. However, I can think of less risky ways to keep your guests amused.

Scented candles have become all the rage and I'm of two minds about them. In the old days all the great hostesses used Rigaud candles, which had a pleasant but noncommittal smell. Now there are so many with really nauseating scents that you have to be careful. Burn a candle first before a party to see if you like the smell, and put it somewhere out of the mainstream so your guests don't feel as if they've been hit with an incense burner when they walk into the room. And please keep them out of the dining room.

I have a very keen olfactory sense and I can't stand to be around strong perfumes or scents of any kind. What I really can't stand is having a heavy scent around me when I'm eating. It interferes with my sense of taste and I can't enjoy my food. I find it rude when women wear overpowering perfume. I feel somehow that my territory has been invaded. I feel that way about overwhelming scents in general. Just keep it subtle if you want to use scented candles, or wear perfume, for that matter.

The smell of fresh flowers, on the other hand, is wonderful. I love walking into a room and having the aroma of lilies come wafting over me. Lilacs are lovely too, and any flower that has a scent adds to the atmosphere of the room. The only thing I would say is keep heavily perfumed flowers off the table. Gardenias, for instance, are sometimes overwhelming and, for those who have a strong sense of smell, could really ruin the dinner.

There's an old religious festival called Candlemas which is celebrated in the darkest time of winter, February 2. The idea is to celebrate the approach of spring as the days are growing visibly longer. You are supposed to light as many candles as you can to keep out the dark, and to adorn the house with flowers to welcome in the growing season. I love the whole idea of Candlemas, the idea of warmth and light and beauty. I'd like all of my parties to feel that way.

There's something about flowers, like fires, that makes you feel welcome. They are beautiful and festive and say, "I've made an effort because you are special." But flowers are expensive. I still think, though, that if you are going to have a party you need to have at least one live flower. A single rose in a vase, a couple of daffodils, a branch of flowering quince, sprigs of holly—anything, really, that's pretty. I personally like seasonal flowers. I like mums in the fall, poinsettias at Christmas, and tulips in the spring. Clichéd, maybe, but they're popular for a reason. Roses are nice all the time. They seem to transcend the seasons. I don't like arrangements; they always seem contrived and unnatural. And I don't like dyed flowers. I love flowers to look as if they were picked in the garden and casually arranged in a vase (I say "vase" that rhymes with "faze," not "vase" that rhymes with "blahs," though both are OK) as naturally as possible.

If someone sends me an arrangement I often take the flowers apart and redo them so that they look as if they had just been picked. I have a garden and for almost nine months of the year we have something we can bring into the house. If you're a gardener it can give you an enormous amount of pleasure, make your house beautiful, and save a lot of money. My most hated flower is the bird-of-paradise, that red plastic-looking thing with a yellow stamen. I also can't stand dyed carnations, particularly dyed blue carnations.

My favorite flower is the peony, especially the pale blush pink ones. They remind me of my son, who was born on April 29, the beginning of peony season. I can't tell you how much joy I got out of those luscious elegant flowers (not to mention my new baby) in the weeks after he was born and how much they remind me of that happy time.

Plants are great, too, and can be very economical as well as long lasting. Orchids are the most expensive and they are beautiful, but you don't get as much bang for your buck. Some of them can be quite leggy and stringy looking, and they often have small flowers that are barely recognizable. Some chrysanthemum plants have glorious colors in fall, and azaleas and camellias are heavenly in the spring.

For me, the idea of flowers in season has such an ordered and satisfying feeling—like having turkey at Thanksgiving and shad roe in spring—that I feel somewhat jolted when I see flowers that don't belong in the season. I don't want vases of beautiful budding pink dogwood in October. I once saw a fatuous interview of a very famous Washington hostess who proclaimed that she always wanted her house to look like a garden in springtime, and the only thing I could think was, why?

This will thrill some and terrify others, but the hostess, usually more than the host, is part of the setting. This can be scary to the guests too, considering some of the getups I have seen over the years. But the fact that there is a certain type of clothing called a "hostess gown" does give one pause. I'm of the theory that a hostess can wear what she feels like as long as it's not over the top and doesn't make the guests feel uncomfortable. A partially nude or scantily clad hostess, for instance, is not a good idea. I've always loved that song which goes, "It's my party and I'll cry if I want to." I'm not in favor of hostesses sobbing in the middle of their parties, but I do feel that a hostess has some leeway when it comes to clothes. For instance, she can wear a long skirt even if the other guests are in casual clothes, or pants if they are in dresses, or a caftan if she chooses.

One Washington hostess who was often featured in *Vogue* and *Women's Wear Daily* used to dress to match her decor. But she got so bored with the same-color clothes she would then be forced to redecorate every few years so she could change the color scheme of her wardrobe. First it was mint green, then a soft peach, and so on. She even insisted on having her hors d'oeuvres match her clothes and her rooms. Once, at a cocktail party, one of her waiters tripped and fell, spilling a tray of hors d'oeuvres all over the living room floor. "Oh, thank God they're all the same color. They won't show!" she exclaimed.

You can carry this to extremes, obviously, but I will say that it can sometimes be jarring to walk into somebody's house that is all done up in pastels and floral chintzes and see the hostess in a garish black, fuchsia, and orange geometric print. You don't have to match the room, but it is nice to look as if you're in the right house.

Another Washington hostess used to insist on wearing ball gowns to her dinners, which were invariably billed as informal. This always made the other women, who were usually dressed in little suits or short dresses, feel as though they had worn the wrong thing.

I'll never forget a day I spent at the Long Island estate of Bill and Babe Paley years ago, when I was in my early twenties. The Paleys were the epitome of power, wealth, and fame. He was the founder of CBS and she was his glamorous, Best Dressed socialite wife. I was going out with Babe Paley's nephew, and we were invited to lunch. I was, of course, somewhat intimidated about what to wear. I chose a black sleeveless linen dress with beige trim around the edge of the collar and armholes. It was simple and basic and good looking, but to my embarrassment she was in pants and a cashmere sweater. I managed to get over that and we were having a rather pleasant time, when we were asked to stay to dinner. I had brought no luggage or change of clothing, so I just assumed everyone would stay in the same clothes for dinner. We gathered for cocktails sometime around 7 P.M., and to my horror Babe appeared in a long dress in some sort of taffeta, and as I recall, Bill Paley wore a smoking jacket and velvet or needlepoint slippers. I was totally mortified and I will never forget that experience and the valuable lesson I learned from it.

The basic rule of being a host or hostess is the Golden Rule. I've said it before and I'll say it again—make your guests comfortable.

There are some men who can carry off traditional host attire, but not many. By this I mean smoking jackets, velvet slippers, and ascots. Now that I think of it, actor Clifton Webb is the only man who comes to mind who could get away with that today. (I guess

Bill Paley did that night at his house.) I once gave my husband an ascot for Christmas, which he reluctantly tried at our next party. For one thing, he didn't know how to tie it right and the thing slid halfway around his neck before the evening had barely started. This was not a great look, not at all suave, and the ascot is now history. My husband will use any excuse not to wear a tie, so he has recently decided a turtleneck will do for almost all social events at our house, especially if it's Sunday night. His rationale is that he is the host and he can wear what he wants. I have long since given up arguing, so I just compromise and buy him decent-looking Ralph Lauren turtlenecks.

Actually, as much as I might complain, when guests arrive and find Ben in a turtleneck, the men seem to relax and it's somewhat of an icebreaker. He particularly likes it because all the men admire him for standing up to me and not allowing himself to be "pussywhipped," as he would say, into wearing what I want him to wear.

(I once read in a magazine that you can always tell when a couple is about to break up or when they have a dysfunctional marriage because when they go out they always look as if they are dressed for different parties. I often wonder what people think of us.)

Sometimes Ben goes too far, though.

The morning of Andrea Mitchell and Alan Greenspan's wedding, I came downstairs dressed in my full Sunday-go-to-meetin' outfit—pale blue suit, chiffon scarf, pearls, high heels, the works. There was Ben in his khakis, a tweed jacket, and a turtleneck.

"You're not wearing that?!" I exclaimed in dismay.

"I certainly am," he said, sticking out his chin in his most foreboding way.

"But this is a wedding!"

"But it's in the country."

"But it's in the fanciest country inn in America!"

"There'll be plenty of people in turtlenecks."

"There will not be one person in a turtleneck!"

(I'm the one with the exclamation marks.)

"Five thousand dollars," he says threateningly, sticking out his right hand, "that there are other people in turtlenecks."

"You gotta deal, pal," I say, and we shake.

For some reason he decided he would change and came back downstairs looking very handsome in a dark suit, white collared shirt, and tie.

When we got to the Ritz-Carlton Hotel, where a bus was waiting to take the guests out to the wedding, Ben mentioned our little contretemps to Jim Lehrer, who gleefully went up and down the bus telling everyone, including Colin Powell and David Brinkley, "You won't believe what that dumb sombitch wanted to wear this morning!"

Ben couldn't stand it and plotted to have the driver stop at Sonny's Surplus on the way to buy a turtleneck for someone, anyone, to wear so he wouldn't have to shell out five thousand smackers to me.

Finally, when Bill Safire got on the bus, Ben, desperate, asked him if he would wear a turtleneck to the wedding for a thousand dollars.

"Sure," said the jovial Safire.

Unfortunately for Ben, the stop at Sonny's was vetoed by the other riders. But never mind. He ended up not being embarrassed and not insulting the bride and groom by being improperly dressed.

He still owes me the five thousand bucks.

That story reminds me of a black-tie dinner in New York, at Sardi's, for the New York Film Critics Circle Award. Alan Pakula was receiving the award for best director and best film for *All the President's Men*, the movie based on the book about Watergate by Bob Woodward and Carl Bernstein. We were all seated at the table, including Jason Robards, who had played Ben, the women in evening clothes, the men in dinner jackets, when in walked Robert Redford to join us in, I believe, jeans, cowboy boots, and a fringed jacket. All I could think of was that if he'd had his wife with him, that never would have happened.

The thing is that, regardless of whether or not it seems important, there is a reason for some sort of conformity in dress. This is not meant to stifle individuality or creativity. Abiding by the dress code simply makes everyone feel more comfortable. And isn't that the objective?

I don't have black-tie parties unless it is a very special event, like a major birthday, anniversary, or New Year's Eve. I kind of think that if you're going to have a black-tie dinner then you should have dancing. That's not a rule, just a feeling.

Parties where special clothing is dictated are in general a bad idea, although there are exceptions. Truman Capote's famous black-and-white ball for Katharine Graham, in November of 1966, was inspired. The dress code gave the party an extra energy and was really no hardship, since everyone owns something that's either black or white. And for the men it was a no-brainer.

I've been to summer parties where everyone was asked to wear white, and that's OK too, and it looks quite pretty to walk in and see a cloud of white against a blue sky and green lawn. Nora Ephron once had a bridal shower for me and all the "ladies" were asked to wear hats and gloves. That was funny, and everyone enjoyed hamming it up. As long as people don't have to go out and buy something special or expensive for the party, I think it's OK.

Costume parties are very risky. In general I hate them because they are so much trouble and can be extremely expensive if you really take them seriously. If someone is having a Renaissance party or an Eighteenth Century party or a Bacchanal, you really do have to rent something or have something made. It can get very competitive and rather tiresome. I think the last costume party I went to was in my twenties. I hadn't given it much thought, so at the last minute I went as a brick wall. I wore a red leotard and drew blocks on it to make it look authentic. My date wore overalls, carried a trowel, and went as a bricklayer. Get it? At any rate, I felt like a fool and my date spent the whole evening chasing after a beautiful dark-haired girl who had come as a flamenco dancer.

Years ago, several friends and I got together to have a costume party on the barge that is pulled by donkeys up and down the C&O Canal here in Georgetown. We had it on Bastille Day, July 14, and asked everyone to dress as if they were stepping out of Renoir's *Luncheon of the Boating Party*. This didn't require much ingenuity. The women wore pretty white blouses, long skirts with sashes, and straw hats. The men wore light suits or shirts with string ties. It was a beautiful day, we had lots of wine and bread and cheese, and a great time was had by all.

The main thing is for you and your guests to dress appropriately. If you're having a cookout, shorts and jeans or sundresses are usually accepted attire. If it's a costume party or a black-tie event or whatever, just make sure guests are informed. Nothing makes people feel worse than to arrive at a party and feel out of place. A good host or hostess should not let that happen.

One last word about the setting. If you are having an unseated buffet supper, either you must have enough chairs and sofas for people to sit on or you have to have soft, thick rugs so they can sit comfortably on the floor. I'm not crazy about bare floors anyway, but you can't expect people to sit on them and eat dinner, even in the summer. It's just not welcoming. I have lots of buffets and I'm not happy unless people end up sprawled all over the floor.

I was so flattered one New Year's Eve when a guest surveyed the scene sometime after midnight and remarked that my living room looked like Coney Island on the Fourth of July.

CHAPTER 9

The
Table

One option is to get the men to change seats midmeal. . . . To
work out this seating requires the ingenuity of a math whiz.

Assuming you're not having a buffet supper, the table becomes the most important thing about your party, after the guests. This is where it happens. This is where hosts' and hostesses' reputations are made or broken.

Relax, I'm only joking. But . . . if it doesn't work at the table, it's over.

Round tables are best for conversation. That's just a fact. Even with twelve people you can have a group conversation with a round table. This does not mean that you have to have a round table to have a successful party. In fact I don't have a round table in my dining room in Washington. I do, however, have a rectangular table that is almost like a round table, where I can have a cozy group of four or ten. My problem is that when I put a leaf or two in the table it suddenly becomes too long for a group conversation and doesn't really work. I can see my way around this problem. I don't like round tables for fourteen—I think they're awkward—so I make the best of the situation when I have more than ten. Usually, if I'm having more than sixteen to eighteen for dinner, I take the dining room table out and bring in several old round fold-up caterer's tables, put skirts on them, and that always seems to work better. The worst tables, and I've fallen for this in a country house once, are those long narrow antique wooden refectory tables. For some reason they are conversation killers. At least those at the end of the table have a little threesome, but those stuck in the center always seem to get left out. I think of those tables as lean and mean. The rounder and more generous a table, the better time guests generally have.

You don't have to have down-filled armchairs at the table, but chairs should be relatively comfortable. Forget backless benches. They may be quaint and look good in the decorating magazines, but you simply cannot have a good time for a whole evening if you can't lean back and relax. Those bamboo upright caterer's chairs don't look it, but they are surprisingly comfortable, especially with cushions, and they don't take up a lot of space, so you can squeeze more people in if you have to. I much prefer to have too many people at the table than too few. It is deadly to have great, huge spaces between seats at a party. A five-foot round table is a good size because you can put four people or twelve at it. Twelve is a little tight, but I find people have a good time when they're jammed in together. The caterers will tell you you can't possibly fit twelve at a five-foot round. They are wrong, but ten is best for that size table. A four-and-a-half-foot round will seat ten, and a four-foot round will do eight. So if you're hard up for space, squeeze 'em in.

I went to a dinner several years ago at the Japanese embassy. The dining room is enormous and the table is the biggest I've ever seen. I think it could easily seat forty or fifty people, and it is so wide that I couldn't see the people on the other side without my glasses. This was a dinner for about eighteen people. Unfortunately, instead of using small round tables, they opted for the big one. Everyone was so spread out that I could barely touch my dinner partner with my arm spread out. On my right was an embassy staffer who spoke very poor English and was so self-conscious about it that he whispered all night. In order for me to make myself understood to him I had to yell. He was at the bottom of the table, and there was nobody on the end. On my left was a former U.S. senator, who is delightful but hard of hearing. It would have been terribly funny if it hadn't been so painful. There was no possibility of having a private conversation, and the public one was embarrassingly inane.

"Wonderful weather we've been having, isn't it?"

"What's that you say?"

"*Wonderful weather . . . ,*" you yell.

Well, you get the picture.

Needless to say, this evening did not pass the Sally Quinn test for successful party giving. The only saving grace was that the sushi was great, so I finally gave up, which I hardly ever do, and just ate.

People like to be in the same room. One of the worst dinners I've been to was a dinner at the home of another Washington hostess (who should know better) with three tables in different rooms. It was so forlorn and gloomy and depressing in each of the rooms that people kept lowering their voices as if they were in church. She could have moved furniture into another room so that all the tables could have been in the same one. The biggest problem was that the rooms were not connected, so it was as if there were three different parties going on.

This doesn't mean you can't have tables in different rooms if you're having a large party, although I do think it makes a difference if the rooms connect.

If I'm having a large dinner party I might have two or three tables in the dining room and two more in the library, but the rooms are next to each other so you can see and hear the other people in the next room. Once, for our tenth anniversary, I even had two tables in the hall, but again, it connected. People want to be where the action is. It's so demoralizing to be at one table in one room and hear raucous laughter coming from another room and feel that you're at the wrong party.

When you walk into the dining room or wherever you're going to be eating, the initial feel of the room as well as the look of the room is extremely important. You want to feel welcomed. Part of what makes you feel that way is the sense that the host and hostess have made an effort for you. The table should beckon you, not push you away. It should seem warm and inviting, not cold or austere.

I happen not to like glass, marble, or chrome tables for that reason. Again, they may look good in decorating magazines, but they don't feel good. They're hard and cold. I suppose if you live in the tropics they're OK, and wrought iron and glass tables in the summer are fine. I even have a problem with polished wood tables with place mats. They look beautiful but they don't feel as nice as cloth. I have a beautiful wood dining room table and often I will use place mats. The table always looks good but I'm never as comfortable with it as I am with a cloth. There's nothing softer or cozier looking than a pretty tablecloth. This is my own personal preference.

There are so many different kinds of tablecloths that infinite variety is possible. There are no rights or wrongs here except for taste. I have some pretty embroidered ones and some linen ones and damask ones, and even a couple of beautiful Porthault table-cloths I got for wedding presents. But I have to say that one of my favorites is a flowered one I had made from a sheet. Everybody uses sheets for tablecloths. Katharine Graham uses sheets. They can be beautiful and festive and they are also inexpensive compared to fancy linen. If you're having a large party and you want matching tablecloths, then getting a bunch of sheets in the same pattern is practical and economical. If you're really imaginative there are many other possibilities. I have one friend who uses thin Moroccan rugs as tablecloths, and they are different and effective. In the end, though, and this is probably heresy to all the professional party planners, nothing could be prettier or more elegant than a simple white tablecloth, flowers, and candles.

Napkins should be very large and generous. I also like them soft. I can never understand why hosts and hostesses want to use starched napkins. They have no absorbency, they slide off your lap, and using them is like trying to dab your lips with waxed paper.

If you're using old caterer's tables or even if you're using wooden tables and are putting cloths on them, you should put some kind of felt or table cover underneath the cloths so it's softer and more comfortable to lean on than a hard, sharp surface. Though the etiquette books say you're not supposed to put your elbows on the table, of course everyone does, especially if it's a successful party and people are leaning in to talk to one another. Again, this is just another little detail to help make your guests have a more pleasurable time.

We've already discussed lighting in general. In the dining room it should be even softer than in the rest of the house. I use only candlelight in my dining room for parties, and if you have enough, the light is perfect. On the tables I usually use votive candles because they are short, or I will use single candlesticks, which add a dimension to the table and look more elegant. I think silver candelabras are beautiful, but if they're too big and interfere with the conversation, they belong on the sideboard. The whole point of having a dinner is to have people talk to one another, and if they can't see one another, that defeats the purpose. Put your pretty candlesticks on the mantel or side tables, cover the dining room table with votives, and you'll have the same effect, and the guests will actually have some idea who's across the table from them.

The same goes for flowers. Have tall flowers anywhere in the dining room except on the table. I have been at dinner parties where I wanted to take a baseball bat and knock the bloody flower arrangement off the table. What can people be thinking when they've got some huge, tall arrangement in the middle of the table that precludes any possibility of communication with the people on the other side of it? I have actually been known to stand up at the table to address someone on the other side of the arrangement. I was trying to make a point. No, I don't think I ever was asked back.

Once I got in an argument with a florist about the height of table arrangements, and after I had sent the flowers back twice I got out a measuring tape and concluded that no arrangement on a table where you have any hopes for conversation should be taller than eleven inches. Am I the perfect little hostess, or what?

As I've said before, you don't need to spend thousands on flowers, especially now that you know you can't have large bunches of flowers on the table. I have some very pretty little blue-and-white Chinese vases about two inches tall, which I can put two or three flowers in. I spread them around the table with the candles and other little pieces of blue-and-white porcelain and it really looks beautiful. It's simple, elegant; it doesn't cost a fortune. And it's low.

This is not to say that you shouldn't have flower arrangements on the tables. (I just don't like formal arrangements *except* on the table.) I do them or have them done all the time, sometimes in little baskets, sometimes with evergreens and ivy, sometimes with flowers and fruit. It's just that you and flower designers (as opposed to florists) can really get carried away with table designs and they end up looking overdone and self-conscious, or "twee," as one of my friends calls them.

Here's the thing about table decorations. You obviously want your table to look beautiful, and it will if you take some care. But you can make yourself crazy if you read too many of these entertaining books about the hostess who spends weeks making the table decorations. The table doesn't have to be "designed" or perfect. Too many people get paralyzed at the idea of not being able to create the perfect setting and end up never entertaining, because they feel insecure. This is ridiculous. You can make cranberry wreaths until your fingers bleed, stencil gold angels on everything that doesn't fly until you're blind, stamp out cookie-cutter hors d'oeuvres and biscuits until the end of time, and it won't make any difference at all if you don't have fun. Things don't make parties. People make parties. If the people don't work, the party won't work, no matter how many weeks you spend making ornaments and decorations.

I happen not to be terribly creative in this department, and it doesn't seem to slow me down. I find that I would rather put my time to good use concentrating on the dynamics of the party than actually spend three weeks making papier-mâché floral sculptures.

It's one thing if you are incredibly artistic and creative and get enormous pleasure out of making things or if you do it professionally and people expect it of you. But the decor-maven host or hostess is in danger of becoming just as much of a bore as the professional-cook host or hostess and the wine-snob host or hostess. If the guests are required to spend more than about five minutes admiring your handiwork, forget it. Remember, the party is not about you. It's about your guests.

Let's talk about the seating. Again, this is not meant to cause undue anxiety, but—sorry about this—the seating is everything. If a person has a bad seat, that person is not going to have a good time. Period. Happily, one person's bad seat can be someone else's idea of paradise, otherwise you'd never have a successful party. Look at the people other people marry.

I'm being a little facetious here, but the fact is that if you're having a party for people who are busy and have a lot of social obligations, spending an entire evening suffering through an excruciatingly boring conversation just isn't worth it. People would rather stay home, eat lightly, not drink, be with their kids, read a good book, watch television, and get a good night's sleep. If they get burned once (and, certainly, twice) they will assume that your house is not what we call a "safe" house (more about that later) and they won't come back.

One friend of mine calls a really tough seat at dinner, with bad partners on both sides, the "gristle" seat. Try never to have a gristle seat at any of your dinner parties.

I happen to like the idea of seating charts. Those are the little leather charts with the shape of the table, either round or rectangular, that stand up like picture frames and are usually placed in the entrance hall or foyer so that you can look and see where you're seated. A lot of people find them pretentious, and I must admit I don't use them all the time. But whenever I see them I am always grateful. What it does is save you from spending the entire cocktail hour talking to the person you're going to be seated next to at dinner. Now you may laugh, but think about it for a minute —especially if it's somebody really boring. If you have ever spent the cocktail hour stuck in a corner with somebody tedious and then ended up seated next to him or her, you know what it means to contemplate either suicide or murder. Even if it's somebody great, somebody you are dying to talk to, you don't want to use up all of your good stories on him or her before dinner. Also, I think there's something sexy about knowing you're sitting next to some-body attractive at dinner and ignoring him during cocktails. It's like a little minuet. It's fun. And it heightens the anticipation of having a good time.

If I'm having a party without seating charts and I see two people in a corner during the cocktail hour who I know will be seated next to each other, I always go up to them and tell them they'll be sitting together. They always make a joke about "Oh, well, we can't possibly talk to each other before dinner," but they invariably look grateful and separate immediately.

Speaking of the cocktail hour, it should be forty-five minutes long. If you invite people for eight you should start mentioning dinner at eight forty-five. The truth is that nobody ever gets to the table until at least nine, but you need to start in that direction after forty-five minutes. I think an overly long cocktail hour kills a party. After a while people begin wandering aimlessly around, looking at their watches. No matter how scintillating your guests

are, the very nature of the cocktail hour precludes any really serious conversation, and you can't sustain polite, superficial chitchat
for much longer than an hour. It just doesn't work. What if everyone hasn't arrived? Too bad. Why inconvenience all your other
guests because of one person? Eat anyway. Presumably such guests
will have called to say they will be late, or else they had better
have been in a serious accident. What if people have just arrived
and want a drink? Let them take their drink to the table or wait
until they sit down and have some wine.

Let's take the worst case. What if it's the President and he's
late? The Secret Service will be there and will advise the host or
hostess how much longer it will be. If the guests have been there
since eight and it's nearing ten, my advice would be to say to the
Secret Service, "I'm sure the President would like us to go ahead
and sit down." That may not be what the protocol office would
advise, but then, I don't have official parties. I've actually been to
a private dinner in Washington where the President was over an
hour late, and the cocktail hour was interminable. Everyone was
hungry, tired, bored, cross, and slightly boozed by the time he got
there, and it was not a great start to the evening.

OK, so now we've gone into the dining room and we're
looking for our seats. Even if you don't have seating charts, and
most people don't, you really should have place cards or at least
tell people where to sit. People don't like to wander around trying
to decide where to sit. It makes everyone feel insecure. You don't
want to appear to be a social climber by grabbing the seat next to
the guest of honor or the most important or famous person there.
You don't want to get stuck with a total dog. You don't want to
impose on a group if there are several friends who have taken seats
at a table and you're not part of it. And if you don't know a lot of
people at the party, then you don't know where you want to sit, or
don't want to sit, for that matter. So it's a real crapshoot. Even if

I'm not crazy about my seat at a dinner party I'd still rather be told where to sit than scramble around trying to avoid a potential disaster and feel like a personal failure if I end up badly.

I always keep a supply of place cards on hand to use if I'm having more than eight people for dinner. I just can't remember where everyone is supposed to sit if I don't have place cards. Sometimes I'll just write down where everyone is sitting and keep the paper in my pocket so I can direct people to their seats. I can't stand the confusion in some houses, where everyone walks expectantly into the dining room and the hostess gets this vacant look on her face and says, "Now, let's see, where did I put you, Ernestine? Oh dear. I'm so confused. I guess you can just sit anywhere." No. No. No. The guests want you to be in charge.

You don't have to have designer place cards either. I just use simple white or ecru ones you can buy in any paper store. But some friends of mine are clever about using old postcards or museum postcards or miniature painted pictures. Polly Kraft, who's an artist, gathers stones from the local pond by her house and paints people's names on them for summer dinner parties.

Whom to put where?

I try not to put people who are close friends next to each other unless it's a tiny party and I have no choice. I think dinners are much livelier if people are getting to know one another for the first time. Putting close friends together is like putting married couples together.

In Hollywood they put husbands and wives next to each other. I've never understood this practice. I think it really kills a party. If I want to sit next to my husband at dinner, I'll stay home. What's fun about going out to dinner is sitting next to someone interesting and then being able to share the conversation with your husband on the way home. The problem with seating husbands and wives together is that you have two different levels of conversation going on at once, and one of them doesn't work from a party standpoint. If husband and wife are talking to each other they're talking about very personal, intimate things, like the car needs a new set of tires and did Junior get his science homework done. The practice also makes it impossible to "turn the table" (talk to the person on your other side), because when it's time to turn, people are faced with having to make party conversation with their spouses for half the evening. And the fact is, they just don't do it. So you end up with awkward three-way conversations.

Ben and I went out to California a few years ago and were asked to a dinner with a lot of actors and producers and directors, all of whom we were interested in meeting. When we went to dinner, we found that all the spouses were seated next to each other. We mutinied and explained that we didn't fly three thousand miles to Hollywood just to sit next to each other. So they put us in between different people, but all the other spouses sat together. We both had a great time but we found that all of our conversations were with two spouses on one or the other side of us, not with one dinner partner on either side. I've never really found anyone in L.A. who can give me a good explanation for this practice.

If I have more than one dinner table I will put spouses at different tables, and if I have two different rooms I'll try to put them in different rooms. I think it increases the sexual energy of a party to have spouses sitting apart.

Sexual energy is a big element of a good party. One of the ways to get it is to have an equal number of men and women. I always try to do girl-boy-girl-boy seating at dinners. I try very hard to have an equal number of each sex so a woman doesn't have to sit next to a woman and two men don't have to sit together. This seems not to be a politically correct notion these days. More often than not you will have more extra women than men, and die-hard feminists don't like the notion that two women shouldn't sit next to each other—though I've found that most die-hard feminists actually like sitting next to men. The theory is that it shouldn't matter as long as the person is interesting. Well, I'm sorry, but it does matter. It changes the dynamics. If you end up with three men sitting together or three women at a table it just seems to go flat. It drains the sexual energy. This is all very subtle, but people don't show off for each other the way they would if they were seated next to someone of the opposite sex. They don't flirt, they don't tease, they don't have the same kind of conversations. It doesn't mean that you're going to go to bed with your dinner partner. It simply makes for a very different party, and in my mind not as successful, if you seat same sexes together. It doesn't mean that you're not going to have a good time. Of course if the people are nice and fun and intelligent you will have a perfectly pleasant time. It just ain't the same.

I will go to considerable lengths to find an extra man or an extra woman to fill in when I don't have an equal number of both. I do draw the line at convicted criminals, religious cult members, and people with the Ebola virus. There are exceptions, of course, but I feel strongly that you have to maintain standards.

Seating according to protocol is obviously much more of a problem in Washington or any world capital than it is in most places. Still, since I don't have official parties, it rarely affects me. In an earlier incarnation, before I became a reporter for the *Washington Post*, I was the social secretary for Algerian ambassador Cherif Guellal. Cherif was young, only thirty-two at the time, single, gorgeous, glamorous, and extremely gregarious and sought after. He lived in Lyndon Johnson's former estate, the Elms, and he loved to entertain, so I spent a lot of time planning parties and doing the seating. I also spent a lot of time on the phone with the protocol office in the State Department, which had a whole staff just to help embassies avoid world crises and wars by not making seating mistakes.

From this job I learned the rules, but one of the most valuable things I learned was when you could break them.

There are a few obvious rules. Even if it's not an official party, if you have the President of the United States for dinner he goes on the hostess's right. The secretary of state, he or she, goes on the hostess's or host's right. The governor of a state, if he or she is the highest ranking, would be on the host's or hostess's right, depending on the sex. The same for the mayor of a city. The reason for protocol is the same as the reason for manners: to make other people feel good. No guest would be offended if the person of obvious rank or stature is given the seat of honor. In fact, to give ranking guests a lesser seat would not only make the persons themselves uncomfortable, but would probably make the other guests feel uncomfortable too.

Generally, I like to spread the wealth by sprinkling the star guests around the table or tables. If I have several tables I will put a VIP at each one so everyone will feel as if he or she is at the most desirable table. What you can't do is put all the stars at one table and everybody else at another. This is rude and hurtful to the people who get left out, and embarrassing for the stars. And it's not going to make for a successful party.

If you have three tables and you put the hostess and guest of honor at one table and the host and guest of honor's spouse at another, then you have to put a star guest or several star guests at the third table to make those people think they are not chopped liver. Otherwise you have what is known in the hostess trade as the "children's table." Nobody wants to be at the children's table, and if it is obvious, it only serves to insult people and hurt their feelings.

I remember a Washington party several years ago in the summer where the would-be host and hostess had six tables, five on their porch and one inside the house. The tables were numbered, with the numbers actually sticking out of the flower arrangements. Table number one had all the celebrities: a couple of politicians,

TV stars, high-profile journalists, and a movie star or two. Table
two had their spouses. Table three had the second-rung guests,
table four their spouses, table five the third-rung guests, and table
six—you guessed it, the table inside—had the spouses of table five
and any leftover less glamorous guests. I have never seen anything
quite like it before. Nor have I ever seen so many unhappy, insulted, and appalled guests in my life. We might as well all have
been wearing name tags with our respective worth as human beings
written on them. It was shocking. Needless to say, these people,
who were more naive than venal, did not go far in the capital's
social whirl.

If you have one long banquet table, putting the heavy hitters
at the top and everyone else in the middle is called putting people
"below the salt." I think that expression came from the fact that
the salt was in the center of the table. This is one reason round
tables are good, because nobody can be below the salt. Remember,
all of your guests are honored guests. Everyone in your home must
be treated like a celebrity, must be made to feel wanted and special.
If any of your guests feel demeaned, then you are not a good host
or hostess.

One thing that I like to do if I have people who see one
another a lot or who are a bit stuffy, or I want to really spread the
wealth, is to switch seats halfway through the meal. This is rarely
done in Washington because the protocol is such a nightmare just
for the original seating.

One option is to get the men to change seats midmeal, taking
their napkins and wineglasses with them. To work out this seating
requires the ingenuity of a math whiz because you not only have
to work out the first seating arrangement but then you have to
rearrange all the men. On the back of each place card you write
the name of the man that person is supposed to change with and
the number of the table if there are more than two or three tables.

This can get very complicated and it gives me a real headache to work it out. I don't do it unless a friend comes over and helps, because I invariably screw it up. However, it is worth it in the end if you do it right, and it gives the party a special charge if there is any possibility that it might lag. It's also good if there are a lot of people who don't know one another very well because it's a way for everyone to meet as many people as possible.

I did this several years ago. At 9 P.M., as we were being seated, one of my guests, Lorne Michaels, the producer of *Saturday Night Live*, arrived to say that the couple he was supposed to have come with, singer Paul Simon and his date, weren't coming. Knowing what disaster lurked, I quickly tried to figure out what we were going to do when all the men changed seats, but it was too hard, so I went into denial. All I will say is that when everyone got up to move, the dining room looked like an old *I Love Lucy* episode. Confusion was rampant. Men were standing helpless in the middle of the room, with everyone looking to me, the hostess, for guidance. You know what I did? I abdicated. "Sit anywhere you like," I said breezily to my hapless guests and quickly poured myself another glass of wine.

The moral of this story: switching seats is risky business. Do it only if you're confident about your guests, have boned up on your math, and are prepared for the worst.

As strongly as I feel about telling people where to sit, I have to say that a hostess has to have nerves of steel to have a seated dinner in the nineties. You can do it, though. Why do you think they invented Prozac?

In Washington it is particularly hazardous because senators and members of Congress vote late and sometimes don't show up until the middle of the meal, or they come and then leave in the middle, or at the last minute they don't show at all.

Journalists are always dashing off on a breaking story or working late on a deadline, and half the guests are in danger of slipping away to do a commentary on God knows what talk show about some major (or minor) news event. Administration people are constantly being beeped by the White House and have to jump up and down from the table to take calls or leave. This is the most prestigious thing that you can have happen, by the way—to be called from the table because the White House is on the line.

In fact, everybody is being beeped all the time. It's catching. One of my son's friends arrived at his fourteenth birthday party with a beeper. Then there are people who fake phone calls and trips just because they don't feel important if they are always the old reliables, always available.

Whether it's Washington, New York, or Hollywood, or anyplace else for that matter, if you invite celebrities to your party you may have to contend with "movie star disease," which is anathema to seating. For reasons I don't understand, many movie stars or celebrities feel that they can accept a dinner and not show up or come very late with no excuses. I've been to three seated dinners in Hollywood where movie stars who were supposed to be my dinner partner or my husband's didn't bother to show up.

Television producer Norman Lear had a fabulous book party for me in Hollywood when my first novel came out. It was also Norman's first party alone, as he had recently separated from his wife. Norman had the worst case of host jitters I've ever seen. Why, I don't know, since he had planned this party perfectly down to the last detail (more later). He was particularly pleased that Goldie Hawn was coming and was going to be Ben's dinner partner, and he mentioned it several times during the day. You can imagine his distress when Goldie called a half hour before dinner to say that she wouldn't be coming. I've never seen anyone so disappointed.

As it turned out he didn't need to worry. Ben had a wonderful dinner partner and the party was one of the most extraordinary ones I've ever been to. Not only is Norman a brilliant TV producer, but he turned out to have major talent as a host as well. The reason? He really cares about his guests and he has a way of making everyone feel special.

Once, years ago, the late superagent Irving (Swifty) Lazar had a party for Ben and me in Hollywood. I was seated on Irving's right (those who were really friends, or wanted people to think they were, called him Irving, not Swifty). On my right was an empty seat where Warren Beatty, an old friend from the campaign days, was supposed to be. Warren was quite late; he was shooting a movie and was very apologetic when he finally arrived. But Irving went berserk before Warren got there.

"This is the last time I will ever have movie stars to my parties ever again," he fumed. "They never show up, they're rude, they don't care about me, they use me." He went on and on. He wasn't talking about Warren in particular (Warren happens to be a very thoughtful and sensitive guy), he was just letting off steam about a social phenomenon, but I could tell that it was something that really hurt his feelings and caused him a lot of pain.

Of course, the minute Warren arrived, he immediately mollified Irving with his abject apology and charmed him into submission. But when I later asked Irving if he had been serious about celebrities, he said yes.

Yet year after year until he died (he was an agent, after all), he put himself through the ultimate host nightmare—an Academy Awards party at Spago filled with stars, and a seated Academy Awards party at that.

If you invite celebrities just make sure you know them and they are safe, otherwise forget it. The excitement of the other guests if celebrities come is not worth the inconvenience and discomfort of the guests if they don't. And it is the other guests you must be concerned about. This goes back to my earlier advice: don't ever invite anyone into your home who thinks they are doing you a favor by being there.

And speaking of safe, make sure your house is known always as a "safe" house. The phrase comes from the CIA but could easily apply to parties. It was coined by the late columnist Joe Alsop, who once remarked years ago that he wouldn't go back to the Iranian embassy (before the ayatollah) because it was not a "safe" house. What he meant by that is that you never knew whether or not you were going to get a dreadful seat. If I go someplace for dinner two or three times and I have a bad seat, I probably wouldn't go again. Who needs it? If I have one goal as a hostess it's to make sure my house is always "safe."

If you have French service, which means the waiter passes the food (from the left) and you serve yourself, the question then arises, should the hostess be served first? I've always done it this way and so have most people I know, but I've never thought about why. At first it might seem rude. After all, wouldn't it be more polite to serve your guests first?

But it does make sense, for these reasons. The old-fashioned reason is that the hostess is a woman, and ladies go first. That seems OK to me, but I think it's too old-fashioned to follow with all the women at the table first and then go back to the men. (It's also disruptive to conversation.) I suppose, too, that if there were any possibility that the food might be poisoned, then the hostess would act as a sort of taster to make sure her guests don't die.

But mainly I think serving the hostess first makes sense because she can then see the platter and determine that everything is being presented as it should be. Also, if she begins, the guests can watch her to see what she does in case there is anything tricky being served that they may not know how to eat.

There's an old story, which may be apocryphal, about the nervous guest who is eating for the first time at a very fancy house. He is advised by a friend to watch the host and do exactly what he does. All goes well until the coffee is served and the host pours some cream into his saucer and puts it on the floor. The guest follows suit, only to discover to his horror that the host has put the saucer there for his dog.

Superfinancier Warren Buffett tells a hilarious story about going to a very elegant dinner at Katharine Graham's years ago shortly after they had met, when he was still pretty green socially. He was doing fine until they served dessert in a *pot de crème*. Warren, who had never seen a porcelain dessert cup with a top, thought the porcelain top was a part of the dessert and cut into it with his spoon. It didn't budge. He cut at it again. Not a dent. Determined soul that he is, he went at it once more. Finally, much to his embarrassment, Kay leaned over to him and whispered gently in his ear, "It might be easier if you just took the top off." He insists he would still be attacking that top today if she hadn't said anything.

What's on the table is the part that sends so many hosts and hostesses, not to mention party goers, into a state of high anxiety.

Let's talk about the fork.

The angst over the fork can make you crazy, and it's all so unnecessary. In the old days, when the upper classes had full sets of silverware for six or eight courses and used them all, it might have been somewhat daunting. But nobody lives that way anymore, and nobody entertains that way.

There are a very few people who have inherited all that old silver and don't have a clue what to do with it. I'm talking about things like terrapin forks and berry spoons. Actually, it could be quite fun to have an occasional dinner with six or eight friends where you did use it all and actually made it part of the fun, discovering along with your guests "which fork to use." In any case, the party is not about which fork to use or how much fancy silver you have on the table.

There is no mystery about which fork (or spoon or knife) to use and only one simple rule, which if you think about it makes total sense: use the piece of cutlery farthest from the plate and work your way in closer to the plate as you go, course by course. For instance, if the meal begins with a soup you're obviously going to eat it with a spoon, and the spoon will be on the far right. So you start there and work your way in. If the next course is fish and there are two forks on your left, you'll use the fork on the outside and then the next, larger fork for the main course. The dessert spoon and fork are at the top of the plate. If the soupspoon is in the middle of the forks, your host or hostess has made a mistake and you should feel highly superior. Always remember that most people feel insecure about which fork to use, so you're not alone. If you're the host or hostess and you don't know, keep the meal simple and you won't have to worry about it. Besides, if you have a great group and the table is beautiful, the food delicious, and there's plenty of wine, who cares? More anxiety has been wasted on using the right fork than on closing the hole in the ozone layer. Let's get our priorities straight here.

These days the most glasses you'll see at a table is four: a white-wine glass with the first course (small), a red-wine glass (larger) with the second, a water glass, and a champagne glass with dessert. Glasses are like the cutlery; the first ones you use should be closer to you on the right above the plate. Occasionally at a very formal dinner there will be a sherry glass with the first course, but that has pretty much gone the way of the dinosaurs. As I mentioned earlier, more and more people are using water glasses too.

It's important, too, to understand what all this is supposed to be about. In the old days, different kinds of cutlery were utilitarian —using various things for different kinds of food because it was easier. Then it became more about form over function. Now a lot of it is for pretension, or show. The main concern here is that nobody wants to make a fool out of himself or herself by not knowing how to do things correctly. The easiest thing to do is to get one of those etiquette books just to assure yourself that you're not making a terrible gaffe. That way you'll feel more confident and then you can relax and forget it. All I can say is that I've never entertained that grandly, nor does anyone I know.

The question of plastic forks and paper plates comes up quite often these days when you're talking to harried working mothers trying to entertain. There are heavy, substantial-looking plastic cutlery and beautiful, decorative paper plates on the market. I think they're fine in the summer for cookouts or porch parties, and I guess if you're moving into a new place and don't have any real forks, they'll have to do. But if you have silverware of your own or silver plate or even stainless steel, I think you should use it. It shows that you think your guests are special enough for you to make the effort to use your best, or even to borrow it from your mother or a friend if you don't have enough.

Service plates are the plates that are on the table when you sit down for formal dinners and then are removed by the waiter when the first course is served. The point of this, as far as I know, is to make your table look as beautiful as possible when people come into the dining room. But it's totally unnecessary and slows things down without a large staff. We have some beautiful blue-and-white Canton china that my husband inherited, and sometimes I will have that on the table when I have a seated buffet dinner. When people find their places they take their plates and serve themselves. It just looks prettier. I have no idea whether this is a socially acceptable practice according to the etiquette books. But it doesn't matter. It works.

Finger bowls are bowls of water to wash your hands in. My feeling about finger bowls is that you should use them only if you need them or if you are over seventy and have always used them. Again, you have to have a lot of staff for this. The odd thing about finger bowls is that most of the time people use them for show when you don't need them and don't use them when you do need them. It's at the grand dinners where you wouldn't touch your food with your hands that they are most often seen, and at the informal dinners where you're eating everything with your hands that nobody would think of using them.

Here's when you need them: for eating lobster, clams, corn on the cob, fried chicken, barbecued spareribs and hard crabs —though when was the last time you saw a finger bowl at a clambake?

Actually, I do use them when I'm serving lobster, but not the fancy kind, with flowers floating in them and doilies. Those are reserved for when you don't need them. I usually put a slice of lemon in mine.

Here's when you don't need them: when you don't touch the food. Here's how to use them: Take the finger bowl and the doily off the plate when it is set in front of you and put it over to your left so you can put the dessert on the plate. Also remove the fork and spoon from the plate and put them on either side of the plate. Do not leave the doily (usually lace, sometimes paper) on the plate, otherwise you will end up eating it. This has actually been done by unknowing guests. Don't let it happen to you.

People have been known to drink the water in finger bowls, thinking it was some sort of clear soup, particularly if it has lemon slices in it.

There is a story, perhaps apocryphal, about a man at a party who picked up his finger bowl, brought it to his lips, and began to drink. His host, not wanting him to be humiliated, then did the same, and the rest of the guests followed suit. Needless to say, that gesture epitomizes the role of the perfect host.

Often in good restaurants you may be served a sorbet, or sherbet, between the fish and meat courses. Occasionally you will see this in a private house at a very fancy dinner, but not often. This is not dessert. It is a *rinse-bouche* and it is meant to cleanse the palate. Don't ask why dessert is being served in the middle of dinner.

One story that will stick in my mind forever is my father's story about taking a prospective CEO to dinner when he was working for a corporation after he retired from the army. He and the chairman of the board of the company and their wives took this man and his wife to dinner at one of the swellest restaurants in Washington. The man ordered fillet of sole, and when they brought it, the lemon was wrapped in gauze. The poor hapless soul spent half the dinner trying to cut the stapled gauze off the lemon, not realizing that it was there to prevent the seeds from falling out over the fish while letting the juice through.

He didn't get the job. The chairman felt that the gauze episode was disqualifying because the man was unable to handle himself properly in a social situation.

The point of this is that it is important to know how to do things right, not only to save yourself embarrassment but to save others from being embarrassed for you.

The main thing is not to be intimidated by anyone professing to know everything about etiquette. People who try to intimidate others invariably trip themselves up every once in a while, and oh, is it delicious! Once, at a very formal dinner in Washington, I was seated next to a famous Washington columnist. During the conversation, I was holding my fork in my left hand and my knife in my right. I set them down briefly on opposite edges of the plate to take a sip of my wine. The minute I did this, this columnist, who is from an old WASP family, crowed in a loud voice for everyone to hear, "Don't you know better than to leave your knife and fork separated on the plate? You never leave them that way. You place them on the right edge of the plate so that they are together. My mother taught me that your knife and fork should always be married."

Naturally, everyone at the table looked at him as though he had lost his mind. Nobody had a clue what he was talking about. I looked down at the offending knife and fork and it didn't look so bad to me. But I quickly shifted them to their "proper" position, making a major deal of it in order to shame him, much to the general amusement of the table.

It was only later, when the dessert arrived, some sort of gooey soufflé, that he got his comeuppance. He looked at the fork and spoon at the top of his plate and mumbled to himself, not thinking I could hear, "I wonder which one of these I should use."

He still hasn't heard the end of that one, and I doubt seriously whether he has ever tried to correct anyone else's table manners since.

The
Entertainment

At one point the entire party simply levitated, it was that magical.

From my point of view, the conversation is the entertainment for any party. If you can't count on good conversation from your guests, you're in trouble, no matter how much entertainment you have. This doesn't mean you can't hire clowns and jugglers and comedians and magicians and singers and bands or anything else. It just means you shouldn't need them.

The whole idea of conversation as entertainment is especially true in Washington. When Henry James first visited the capital in 1905, he remarked on "the superior, the quite majestic fact of the City of Conversation pure and simple, and positively of the only specimen, of any such intensity, in the world."

The conversation is the responsibility of the host or hostess, at least at their tables or their ends of the table. What this means is that you have to have something to say. It means you need to read the papers and make sure to watch the *Today* show, as I so tactfully pointed out on *Good Morning America,* and other news broadcasts. You don't have to be an intellectual superstar, but you need to know what's going on so you can converse with some knowledge about the events of the day. It's important to do a little homework—to know what's happening in the community, something of general interest, and something about all of your guests, particularly your guest of honor. Has this person written a book or article, or made a movie, or been in a movie? Has that person done a great job raising money for a local charity, or organized a kids' baseball team, or won a prize in the local bake-off? If you know about your guests you can ask intelligent questions, and there is nothing more flattering to anyone than to have others know of their accomplishments.

It is also up to the host or hostess to "turn the table." Presumably you will have started a conversation with your guest of honor or whoever is on your right. There are some schools of thought that say you should start with the person on your left, but I've never heard of a good explanation why, and anyway, it doesn't matter. There is no place for rigidity at a dinner party. Sometimes the person on your right has gotten into a conversation with the person on his right while you were making sure everyone had found his or her place. So you would talk to the person on your left rather than break up the whole table. This means that about halfway through the dinner you need to turn to the person on your other side and begin a conversation. What you do not want to do is stop a conversation in midsentence and turn immediately to your other side. You find a time when there is a natural change of subject or break, then you pull your chair back a bit to include the person on your other side and you say, "We were just talking about . . . ," and bring him into the conversation, thereby allowing the person on your other side to turn to his other dinner partner. It sounds simple, but you'd be surprised how awkward it can be. I plead guilty, too, in getting caught up in an interesting conversation and forgetting to turn the table until I feel a deafening silence on my other side.

Perhaps because I am a journalist, I am almost never at a loss for something to talk about because, I find, I end up interviewing everyone. There's hardly a soul who doesn't have something interesting in his background, even if his grandfather was an ax murderer. Dysfunctional families yield incredible stories, and almost everybody has one.

You ought to prepare yourself by thinking about five or six things that have been in the news recently and that everyone might be interested in. If you can't remember them, write them on a small piece of paper and stick it in your pocket for use if the conversation lags. This may sound a little silly, but whatever works, is the way I look at it. If there's a story about sexual harassment, bring it up. Everyone has different views on the subject, and it will get things moving. Anything to do with sex gets things moving. My personal philosophy regarding dinner party conversation? When all else fails, talk about sex.

I was at a dinner at the French embassy several years ago and I happened to be sitting at the ambassador's table. It was a ghastly group. There were several really boring senators, a boring ambassador, and a member of the French government, plus our new ambassador to France. A total killer. The dinner dragged on—despite the good food—with long silences as people sort of stared into space in between courses. (This was an example of a party where even great food couldn't save the evening.) I was chattering along like a magpie, trying to keep things alive, when finally I couldn't stand it any longer. I brought up the subject of a book about sex recently published in France that had taken the French by storm, and asked the ambassador how he felt about it. Before you could say Rip Van Winkle, the entire table had awakened from their slumber and began arguing and talking animatedly. This lively topic kept us awake until the toasts, at which time everyone nodded off again. (More about toasts later.)

Recently we lent our house to a charity event, and the woman who was hosting the party called to ask me if there was anything interesting or noteworthy about the house or any of the furniture or paintings, because she thought it might be an icebreaker for the guests. I thought that showed a lot of foresight, particularly because there were so many people coming whom she didn't know.

Washington is different from most towns in that politics dominates everything that goes on here, so you really have to keep up with what's going on politically if you want to have any success at entertaining. In New York it may be publishing or the theater or music; in Hollywood, movies; but some version of this is true most places.

It used to be very difficult for women in Washington, who were often overlooked. There was a saying that Washington was full of important, powerful men and the women they married when they were young. And in the old days these women made the dinner parties a challenge for their hostesses and their dinner partners alike.

Katharine Graham's late husband, Phil, had a wonderful expression he used for these women, which, unfortunately, was all too accurate. He called them "fractionalizers." So often at those dinner parties, the men would resort to group conversation in order to avoid talking to the women on either side of them. The women couldn't handle a group conversation, so they would be forced to sit quietly and listen. Occasionally they would try to get back in the game by attempting to speak privately to one of their dinner partners, or by "fractionalizing the conversation."

My husband used to say that if he was sitting next to the wife of, say, the secretary of state, he would come away knowing everything about their children and if I was sitting next to her husband, I would learn everything about foreign policy.

Once, years ago, when it was announced on television that a very distinguished person had been appointed to a cabinet position, my husband began to moan, "No, oh no, I can't stand it."

Why, I asked, was he so upset when this man was such a good choice for the job? "Maybe," he said, "but I'll get his wife at dinner."

The sad thing was that in those days, a lot of these women, nice as they were, simply had no life or interests outside the home and the rearing of their children. Even so, it was expected that the woman's role was to "bring out the men at dinner," asking them questions about themselves and their work—appealing to their egos. If I heard my mother say it once, I heard her say a thousand times, "Let them talk about themselves and they'll think you're brilliant and fascinating." She wasn't all wrong either, my ole mama.

Pity the poor wives, or women in general, who had to spend their entire evening sandwiched between two important, pompous, arrogant, and self-centered men who did nothing but brag about their exploits.

I once had that experience. At a very fancy dinner in Washington I sat between a columnist from out of town and a member of the administration. I couldn't get a word in edgewise, which for me is amazing. Finally I gave up, in disgust, even trying to participate in the conversation, and the minute dinner was over, I fled. About a half hour later the columnist came rushing over to me. "My God," he said, looking alarmed. "I just found out you were Sally Quinn. We must have a talk."

Pulling myself up to full height, I replied with great satisfaction, "Too late, buster," and sashayed off to the other side of the room.

Because things have changed considerably since those days, today it is quite likely that my husband might get the cabinet officer and I get her husband.

It is also likely that almost all the women work or have a career and are just as interesting as, if not more so than, the men. And too, the responsibility for keeping the conversation going is just as much with the man as it is with the woman. Most working women today just won't be bothered to try and draw out their dinner partner or spend the evening listening to some egotistical bore drone on about his opinions. They'll just ignore him. For a man to succeed at a dinner these days he's got to understand that conversation is a two-way street.

Even if you've got talking points in your pocket, I really think you have to be spontaneous. You can introduce a topic, but if it doesn't take off there's not a whole lot you can do about it.

This brings us to the subject of agendas, or seminars, or forced topics at a dinner party. I use the expression "dinner party" deliberately because I don't believe you can separate "dinner" and "party." As I mentioned earlier, the late ambassador to France and Washington hostess, Pamela Harriman, insisted that her dinners have a serious purpose. "I wish the phrase 'dinner party' had never been invented," she once said. "To me a dinner is about something serious. You get substance from a dinner. You learn something. A party is a celebration like someone's birthday. Averell and I far more often have dinners. A dinner has a purpose."

This is totally the opposite of my attitude toward entertaining.

I read once in a magazine about some hostess who was pontificating about her parties, and she said something like, "One *gives* dinners, one *has* parties." Or maybe it was the other way around. I couldn't imagine what she was talking about.

I had the same reaction when I read Pam Harriman's quote. The point of a dinner, a party, or a dinner party is to enjoy yourself. You can also talk about serious things, get substance from them, and learn something. A dinner or party or dinner party can also have a purpose—to celebrate a birthday, congratulate someone for a promotion, pay tribute to someone retiring, or honor someone for whatever reason. But it should still be fun. Life should be fun. Why should dinners be different?

Still, fun for one person may not be a million laughs for another. If you've got a bunch of scientists for dinner and they're talking about microbes and enzymes and particles, they may end up screaming with laughter, throwing food at one another, belting down the tomato juice, and generally think they've had the best time of their lives. Get a group of mechanics together talking about wrenches, mufflers, and spark plugs, and they may feel they've died and gone to heaven. (In order to hold my own here, I would definitely change the topic to sex . . .)

As I've said, Washington is pretty much a one-topic town. I happen to be a political junkie and I could talk for hours about confirmation hearings, campaign financing, Bosnia, or the latest standoff on budget talks. I know all the players, so for me these conversations are as much about the people involved as they are about the subjects. I never come away from a dinner party without having learned something. That for me is fun. But I don't go to a party or, God forbid, give one with the express purpose of having a "serious" conversation or getting "substance" out of it. I take vitamins for that kind of thing.

The historian Arthur Schlesinger was right when he said that "Washington is a city where the most serious purpose lurks behind the greatest frivolity."

Since Washington social events are often working events, in many instances they are simply an extension of the office, only people wear dinner jackets instead of business suits.

In the years I covered parties for the *Washington Post* I always came back with a story, sometimes with news that ended up on the front page. News is often made at Washington dinner parties, even at the most private ones. Even at my house. But work is never the purpose of my parties, and that's the point.

As I've noted, if you are a host or hostess it is tricky to have an agenda for a party unless you announce it beforehand: "We're having a party to introduce our good friend Joe Blow, who has just written a book and is going to give a talk about it before dinner." Or, "We're having a few people over to meet Jane Doe, who is running for office and is going to speak to us during cocktails." Forewarned is forearmed. I don't give these kinds of parties, but I don't object to them as long as I know what I'm getting into.

Wren and Tim Wirth—he's a former senator from Colorado and now undersecretary of state for global affairs, and she's an environmental activist—often have small dinners, for eight or ten friends. They are elegant and fun but there is usually an agenda. They will have some friend who is an expert on population, for instance, whom they will tell you about in advance, and after dinner, while everyone is at the table, Tim will start a conversation on that subject. They always end up having spirited conversations by like-minded people, and everyone ends up having a good time. The point is that you know what to expect.

What makes me crazy is when I'm just relaxing and getting into a good conversation and suddenly there's a tap, tap, tap on the glass and the host announces that we are now going to talk about the Burmese political situation or the latest community immunization program. It's not that I'm not interested in those topics. It's just that I don't want somebody telling me I have to talk about them, especially if I'm not in the mood. That is not fun. And as the former governor of Alabama George Wallace would say, an evening like this would just "bo' yo' ass."

The problem, too, is that these kinds of evenings bring out the worst in people. Even the nicest, most self-effacing people can become self-conscious and pretentious in these situations. And inevitably you've got a bore who really takes himself or herself seriously and becomes even more insufferable when presented with this kind of opportunity. I always come away feeling bad after one of these evenings. Either I've clammed up and feel stupid or I've shot off my mouth and feel like a jerk. If you're going to do this kind of dinner you'd better know your group and have a pretty good idea that everyone will enjoy it. Otherwise, trust good old spontaneous conversation.

I've been to a few evenings like this that have worked, but they have evolved unplanned. One was a dinner during this past inaugural given by the actor Ron Silver. It was a small dinner, twenty people or so, with quite an illustrious guest list. At dessert Silver got up to make a toast and remarked that there were a number of people there who had given something to their country. He started asking people what they thought their greatest sacrifice had been in life. It was completely spontaneous and he ended up going around the table, getting most people to speak. It was remarkably moving and emotional. Among the guests were Gen. Colin Powell and Sen. Bob Kerrey from Nebraska, both Vietnam veterans. Later, however, one of the male guests who had to leave early and missed the experience commented to me about Kerrey, "I'm glad I wasn't there. I don't want to have to talk about my sacrifices when I'm sitting across the table from a war hero who's had his leg shot off and been awarded the Medal of Honor."

I guess because I live in Washington I think that my whole life is a seminar. When I go to a dinner party I want to have a good time. Every once in a while I will accept one of these agenda evenings, though, just because I'm always afraid I'm going to miss something.

One such evening was billed as a "Critical Mass" dinner on the invitation, sent by Arianna Stassinopoulos Huffington, the conservative writer and recently separated wife of unsuccessful multimillionaire senatorial candidate Michael Huffington. *Critical Mass* was the name of a talk show she was trying to get off the ground. When we arrived I was shocked to find that the topic was "Spirituality" and the guest list consisted of probably the ten most savvy journalists in Washington, including Meg Greenfield, Richard Cohen, Charles Krauthammer, and Andrew Sullivan, which is really saying something. This crowd could sniff out hypocrisy better than pigs root out truffles. Things only got worse when everyone discovered she had tape-recorded the entire dinner-table conversation unbeknownst to her guests. As you can imagine, the dinner was an unmitigated disaster for the hostess, and if she had served mud pies the guests would most likely have thrown them at her. On a scale of one to ten, ten being a success—well, you guessed it. And yet, I have to admit, it was one of the most entertaining parties I have ever been to in Washington. There's nothing more riveting than social self-immolation. So . . .

If Huffington had invited a group of New Age people from the West, the evening might have been a big hit. This was a perfect example of not knowing your guests.

Years ago in Washington the tradition of separating the men and the women after dinner was still in full force. I always hated it because I didn't want to miss out on any of the good stuff, having to go upstairs with the ladies for coffee when the gentlemen retired to the library for brandy and cigars. This became particularly galling after I went to work as a reporter for the *Washington Post*.

One night my husband and I were invited to Averell and Pam Harriman's for a dinner in honor of Sen. Frank Church, who was contemplating a run for the presidency. After dinner, Pamela tapped on her glass and announced that the ladies would be joining her for coffee upstairs while the men would be asked into the living room to hear Senator Church discuss his political plans. I had been assigned to do a profile on Senator Church for the *Post* and I was wild at the notion that I was supposed to go upstairs and miss his comments. As the ladies dutifully trooped out of the room behind Pam, and Ben sheepishly, without daring to look my way, slinked into the living room, I followed the men. I intended to tell Ben I was leaving but was stopped by Governor Harriman, all six-feet-something of him. He glared at me, pointed a finger to the stairs, and commanded, "Miss Quinn, the ladies will go upstairs." Before I could respond, he bellowed, "Miss Quinn, this is my house, and in my house the ladies go upstairs after dinner." With that, I said, "Good night, Governor," turned, and walked out of the house.

I, of course, was shaking like a leaf, both amazed that I had done it and still outraged at having been spoken to like that.

The furor that followed was incredible. The story went out over the wires and was in newspapers all over the world. It was reported on radio and television, and my behavior hotly debated in salons all over Washington and New York. After that I never went to another party where the men and women separated, and fairly soon the custom disappeared completely.

It's hard to believe it was only some twenty years ago.

Once dinner is over, if the party is in someone's honor there are likely to be toasts. If they're good, the toasts can be the best entertainment you could have. The host or hostess should always be in control of the toasts. If it's something small, there could be simply a toast by the host, or a toast and a response from the guest of honor. However, if it's a very big deal, like a major birthday or anniversary, there are likely to be many toasts, and the well-wishers, by the time toasting comes around, are very likely to be feeling no pain. If it is a big event, the host or hostess should designate the toasters and keep them to a manageable number. If there are much more than thirty minutes of toasts, you are definitely in the danger zone unless all of the toasters are as funny as Robin Williams.

What you must never do is designate the toasters and then announce that if there is anyone else who would like to say something they can. Totally wrong. This will only encourage the town bore, who will be half in the bag by the time the toasts are over, and really finish off the party for good.

The other thing you must never do is to call upon someone to make a toast who has not been warned ahead of time. This is just not fair, especially if the person is known for giving good toasts and is a good speaker. What usually makes people good at these things is that they work hard at them and prepare them, or at least give them some thought in advance, and you just can't blindside them.

I saw this happen once at a fiftieth-birthday party of a friend. All of the speakers had been designated ahead of time except for one out-of-town friend, who must have been the victim of an oversight. At any rate, after several well-rehearsed and hilarious toasts in front of a very high-powered crowd, the host called on him to make a toast. I've never seen anyone so mortified in my life. Generally an inspired speaker, and a close friend of the honoree, he was practically tongue-tied. He managed to mutter something about having not been prepared and lamely wished the birthday girl a happy second half of her life. But it ruined the party for him, and even now, years later, it's still a painful memory.

My good friend and the brilliant illustrator of this book, Susan Davis, actually did this to me recently at a wedding party for mutual friends, journalists Martha Sherrill and Bill Powers, given by journalists Bob Woodward and Elsa Walsh. We had all been asked to create some sort of meaningful icon for the wedding cake, which I dutifully did. But when it came time for the toasts and the cutting of the cake, Susan, who was acting as master of ceremonies, announced that we would all be explaining the significance of our icons, and "We'll start with Sally first." My icon was obvious and required no explanation, but more important, I, who am rarely speechless, was so surprised that I could only manage to suggest that she continue around the room. Martha turned to Susan and laughed. "You've just made it into Sally's book. "

What you hope for in your toasts is to have people laughing, wiping away a tear or two, and feeling warm and sentimental at the end, ready for another drink.

A note of caution here. Don't ever go around the room and single out people to mention in a toast—"Old Dan has been the best friend I've ever had," "Harry was there when I needed him," "Dottie always made me laugh"—unless you mention everyone. If you want to do one or two or even three, assuming you have a large crowd, fine. But it hurts people's feelings to have half or more than half of the guests singled out for compliments while they sit there on the sidelines. The worst is when men do this, because they inevitably mention only the men, as though the women didn't exist. I've seen this happen so many times and seen it done by otherwise intelligent men. If it weren't so appalling it would actually be funny.

The only person I've ever seen do this perfectly is Elsa Walsh. Ben and I had a coed baby shower/dinner party for Elsa and Bob Woodward after their baby Diana was born. We had two tables of twelve, and Elsa managed in her toasts to go around the room and say something wonderful and, more important, true about every single person there. I held my breath, thinking that she would surely forget someone and there would be hurt feelings, but she was flawless. You should never try this, though, unless you can pull it off the way Elsa did.

One of the things I find curious is how rarely women make toasts. It's almost always the men, even in a crowd where the women are as successful and accomplished as the men. The men seem more comfortable with it and, but for rare exceptions, I'm sorry to say, are often better at it. For one thing, men seem to enjoy roasting the guest of honor, assuming it's another man. Women are much more sincere and sympathetic in their toasts, almost apologetic for taking people's time.

One of the great toasts given by a woman is the toast Lauren (Betty) Bacall gives to my husband on his birthday. Every August in East Hampton, I say I'm not having a party for Ben, and then I wind up having it after all. And I know it won't be complete without Betty Bacall's toast. She gives the same one every year, and every year it seems to get funnier. In her sexiest voice and with her eyelids lowered in her best "Just put your lips together and blow" mode, she delivers this deadpan and has everyone screaming with delight—not to mention my husband, who is inevitably beside himself with ecstasy at the very idea of it. She gives, actually, two toasts, which she thinks she heard from the late New York gossip columnist Walter Winchell. They go like this:

"To your eyes,
To my eyes,

> To your lips,
> To my lips.
> The former have met,
> The latter not yet.
> Here's hoping!"

And the encore:

> "May you live as long as you want to,
> And want to as long as you live.
> If I'm asleep, wake me.
> If I'm awake and don't want to, make me."

The important thing when, as a host or hostess, you are designating toasters is to know them well and to know your crowd. And it's equally important for the toasters to know the crowd.

Every summer at Ben's birthday party, aside from Betty Bacall, I ask two friends, Howard Stringer, former president of CBS and now head of Sony, and Peter Stone to speak. They are the two most brilliant toasters I have ever known and are used to performing in front of very tough, discriminating entertainment types in New York and Hollywood. They are hilarious, and at every birthday party they bring the house down, usually with some sort of roast of Ben.

I invited them to speak at Ben's seventieth birthday at Porto Bello, our house on the St. Marys River in southern Maryland. Both of them did their usual summer roast of Ben. But as they were the first to point out, what would have been a triumph in East Hampton just didn't quite work. Ben had stepped down that month as editor of the *Washington Post* after nearly thirty years, and many of those in the audience were from the *Post*. What Howard and Peter couldn't have known was that there was a great deal of sentimental feeling for Ben that night and the crowd was clearly uncomfortable with the idea of seeing him roasted. It wasn't

Howard and Peter's fault. They just didn't live here and weren't able to gauge the mood of the crowd.

Undaunted, however, both of them used their experience at Ben's birthday to spawn an entire cottage industry of jokes about how they had bombed in St. Marys County. Some of the funniest toasts I have ever heard were toasts they both made later about their performances that night. One night, at the seventieth-birthday party of Don Hewitt, the producer of 60 *Minutes*, Peter actually had people crying with laughter, comparing his toast to Don to the toast he gave to Ben.

Unfortunately, Howard and Peter both felt so burned by the whole thing that now they will give only sentimental toasts to Ben. They keep saying things like what a great American he is. Frankly speaking as a wife, I'd like to see them bring back the roast.

On the other hand, we have another friend, *Washington Post* reporter Walter Pincus, who gives the most unforgettable toasts you have ever heard. Walter is famous for long, rambling, disconnected toasts in which he inevitably insults at least the guest of honor if not half of the other people at the party. Walter's toasts are legendary and everyone looks forward to them because they invite group participation. Before he is finished his audience is laughing, screaming, booing, hissing, catcalling, throwing napkins, and demanding the hook. The worse it gets, the more Walter loves it. Part of the success of the toast is his wife, Ann, putting her head in her hands, rolling her eyes, and moaning with mock despair. This is a local ritual that outsiders have some difficulty understanding. Without group participation Walter's toasts don't work.

One night Walter and Ann, who comes from Little Rock, Arkansas, had President and Mrs. Clinton for a dinner in honor of writer Ward Just and his wife, Sarah, who were visiting from

Martha's Vineyard, Massachusetts. There were only about sixteen of us, and after dinner Walter got up and launched into what I must say was his all-time tour de force. You could see the Clintons looking quite nervous at first and a bit puzzled as the guests began to attack Walter in the middle of his toast. It went on with much hilarity for at least fifteen minutes as the Clintons began to get the joke and relax a bit. Finally, unable to stand it any longer, the late Les Aspin, then secretary of defense, threw his napkin across the table and yelled in as loud a voice as possible to be heard above the din, "Bring it home, Walter, bring it home!"

I don't think Walter will ever top that night. But it illustrates my point that you have to know your crowd.

Now, about the real entertainment.

We've finished the dinner and either we're having coffee at the table or it's being served in the living room. Or not, if it's at my house.

Music is the obvious first choice of entertainment and I'm all for it, except when it interferes with the conversation.

For very special parties some people like to have a combo playing throughout the evening. Just keep them far enough away so you can talk. Others like somebody at the piano in the background. Fine, but the same warning. When I had a harpist at the lunch for Quinn's christening it seemed fitting. After all, he was my little angel!

If you're having dancing and you have a band after dinner, that's fine, because people can drift away if they want to talk. At Ben's seventieth birthday we had a band and a singer (Ben likes to remember her as a "chanteuse" or "thrush") after dinner. Between courses the band played soft ballads and people could dance if they wanted, but you could still carry on a conversation. After dinner the band broke out into livelier music, and those who wanted to let loose on the dance floor could, while others took refuge in the back of the tent.

On New Year's Eve the DJ plays golden oldies, starting at the beginning of the evening with soft jazz and ballads and working up to rock and roll after "Auld Lang Syne." People dance in the hall, and those who don't want to can talk in the adjoining rooms without shouting.

One of the great musical party experiences of my life was at Ben's sixty-fifth birthday party in Long Island. Norman Lear was a guest, and unbeknownst to Ben and the other guests, he had arranged for eighteen or twenty violinists to show up in white tie and white tails. During cocktails one of them emerged from the bushes and started to play, much to everyone's astonishment. Then, five minutes later, another one jumped out of the bushes, and so on until all of them surrounded Ben and played these wonderful tunes. I really do think at one point the entire party simply levitated, it was that magical. And to top it all off, one of the guests happened to be the great violinist Isaac Stern, who grabbed a violin from a stunned musician and played "Happy Birthday" to Ben when they brought out the cake.

One of the most exciting evenings of my life was one summer when I was a teenager. My father took me to a small seated dinner in a Georgetown garden. Surprisingly, I was seated next to Allen Dulles, the director of the CIA. Much to everyone's delight, the host had hired a violinist for the evening, a very unusual thing to do in those days. After dinner the violinist came up to me and asked if I had a favorite song. I asked him to play "La Vie en Rose," which I do think is the most romantic song I know.

"What a brilliant choice," exclaimed Mr. Dulles. "That's my favorite song too!"

I was in total ecstasy. Ever since then I've always loved the idea of violins at parties, which is why Norman's gesture with the violins at Ben's party was so special.

I have been to parties where there have been comedians. Normal Lear actually had the comedian Red Buttons do a stand-up comedy routine about me at the book party he gave for me in Los Angeles for my first novel. Norman doesn't mess around.

Others have had famous magicians entertain their guests after dinner, and last year at a dinner given by the Saudi ambassador, Prince Bandar, for the departing British ambassador, we were all asked into the living room after dinner and treated to a private concert by singer Roberta Flack.

These events are rare and extravagant exceptions, beyond the means of most of us. I mention them just to give an example of the kinds of entertainment that have been really successful.

What could be amusing entertainment for five or ten minutes can turn deadly when it runs over a half an hour. An example of this was a farewell party for Richard Holbrooke when he stepped down as assistant secretary of state during the first Clinton administration. It was given by the Spanish ambassador, a very nice man, at the embassy. There was a large diplomatic crowd. Many of the people didn't know one another, and the dinner itself seemed to go on forever, with many courses and slow service. It was a "school night," and as the toasts were ending, near 11 P.M., everyone was getting desperate to get out of there. But before anyone had a chance to move, the ambassador announced that we would be entertained by a group of flamenco dancers. A soft moan could be heard around the room as a troupe of heavyset ladies of a certain age in garish costumes clunked their way out to a raised platform in the center of the room and began with the castanets and the clicking of heels. This went on and on and on. They would finish one set and people would be on the edge of their chairs, ready to bolt, when they would announce another song. I'm sorry, but I'm not sure this would have been tolerable even to the men if they had had the entire cast of *Baywatch* in skimpy costumes doing flamenco at that hour.

All I can say is that when it was finally over there was a near stampede for the door. Any observer would have thought somebody had yelled "Fire!" Ben and I had caught each other's eye and had managed to beat the mobs by several minutes. But given the scene as we departed, I fully expected to read in the paper the next morning that several guests had been trampled to death in the melee.

There is always a fine line between what is in good taste and what is ostentatious. I think some of the things I've just mentioned are in good taste, mainly because they were unique and gave the guests so much pleasure.

There was one party several years ago that I think went over the line. A New York socialite had a birthday party for her husband. I was not there but read the reports and talked to several guests who were. Apparently she had set up these huge *tableaux vivants*, mini stage sets with live actors, each one portraying a famous painting. The live actors simply stayed still and posed while the guests wandered around and stared at them. This had to be enormously expensive. When the message is "Look how rich we are," it makes everyone else feel bad that they're not. And that defeats the purpose of the exercise, as my father would say.

Games are another matter.

I am not a game player. I just don't enjoy games. I don't like situations where somebody has to lose. My husband thinks I'm from another planet, but there you are. What I really hate is to go to a party and be told, "And now we're going to play . . ." whatever it is. I always feel cornered. If I do play I'm miserable, and if I don't play I feel like a bad sport or a party pooper. This doesn't mean that I never play games. It just means that I want to know about it beforehand so if I'm not in the mood I don't have to come or I can plan to sneak out early without feeling sandbagged.

You have to warn guests or prepare them if you are planning to play games or do anything that requires guest participation (Walter Pincus's toasts excepted).

Actually, Howard Stringer, head of CBS, and his wife, Jennifer Patterson, who is a doctor, had a great party several years ago where they handed out sheet music after dinner with songs about everyone's name and, with musical accompaniment, we all sang tributes to one another. Mine was "Long Tall Sally." That was a lot of fun, and those of us who couldn't sing could just move our lips and nobody knew.

Journalist Martha Sherrill once planned a karaoke evening. Karaoke involves renting a special TV that plays music and has the words of the songs on the screen. You pass a mike around the room so that people can sing, following the music and the lyrics. Martha was smart about it, though. Instead of forcing people to do it or even mentioning it, she just set up the equipment for all to see and waited until after dinner, when the crowd demanded that they be allowed to sing.

"Come for dinner and charades, dinner and poker, dinner and Murder in the Dark, dinner and reading Dickens out loud, Trivial Pursuit, madrigals, Dictionary, bridge, backgammon" . . . anything. You really have to warn people when the games require equipment, like round-robin tennis tournaments or treasure hunts. Give your guests a chance to take a rain check.

The all-time worst dinner-party game was one my parents were forced to play years ago before my father retired. They were asked to dinner by a neighbor. It was a getting-to-know-you kind of thing for the people on their block. After dinner, which my parents reported was deadly, the host and hostess passed around bowls of bubble gum, which they asked all of their guests to chew. After they had chewed it fairly thoroughly and gotten all of the juice out as instructed, the host announced that they should all take the gum out of their mouths and make sculptures with it. The best sculpture would win a prize. Yes, that was the last time my parents went to those neighbors for dinner.

One thing you should be careful of is the idea of having the same party every year. "Oh no, the Schwartzwalders are having their Groundhog Day party again this year" is not the reaction you want when your guests get the invitations. I know, I know, tradition and all that. It's just that after a while everything gets old. This is why, every so often, I don't have the New Year's Eve party, just so people won't take it for granted and it doesn't lose its specialness. I don't know how I decide, but it's usually by licking my finger and sticking it up in the air to test the atmospherics. I'm not saying never, and there are some events that people do look forward to every year and would be disappointed to see discontinued.

Television journalist Sam Donaldson and his wife, TV reporter Jan Smith, have a wonderful Christmas cocktail party every December that is warm and cozy and sort of signals the beginning of the holiday season. I always look forward to their festive invitations because I know the party will be great. But sometimes traditional parties lose their magic and mystery and just aren't fun anymore.

Political consultant Tully Plesser and his wife, cookbook writer Michelle Evans, had a wonderful party every summer in Long Island where they had everyone come prepared with a song to lip-sync to. This was before karaoke was hot. After a delicious supper, they set up a mike, the host played the piano, and everyone got to make an ass out of himself. Some people made up songs; others formed little singing groups. Sheets of music were passed out and everyone sang along to old show tunes afterward. It was terribly funny and a lot of fun. But after a few years it became so popular that people were trying to muscle their way in; the number of guests grew too large, and people actually started hiring singing coaches to prepare them for their performances. The host and hostess finally stopped having it, and they were right. It was fabulous when it began, but in the end it had changed too much and lost its original spontaneity.

Other friends, Gil and Lena Kaplan, had a summer picnic on their lawn, invited a hundred or so friends, and had the Olympic diving team perform by their pool after lunch. As you can imagine, it was incredible the first year. And for several years afterward, everyone looked forward to it. But while it was still at its peak, before people could get tired of it, they stopped. It, too, had run its course.

Oh my God! I just thought of something. What if they're still having these parties, only we're not invited anymore . . . ?

Some people have the misguided notion that their children should be part of the entertainment. Forget it. Grown-ups go to grown-up parties to see other grown-ups. I'm clearly not talking about family events here. The fact is that I love my friends' children and I love to see them.

I think it's fine if the kids come downstairs to greet the guests and get exclaimed over. It's OK too if the kids serve hors d'oeuvres, as long as they really do serve them quietly and politely and then disappear. But remember, unless it's a children's party, then it's not about them, and you are going to bore your guests out of their minds if they have to spend the entire evening complimenting little Horace on how big he is and little Clarabelle on what pretty eyes she has. The problem is, you have to pay attention to them or their parents get insulted. If you really want to show off your kids (how much of this is about them and how much is it about your own ego, anyway?), then have a Fourth of July family cook-out, a Halloween party, or an Easter egg hunt, where the whole purpose is to brag about your kids.

One of my favorite parties was about four years ago, when I didn't have the New Year's Eve party. I decided to have a Christmas party and invite my friends and their children. I set up a gingerbread-making table in Quinn's playroom, and the kids wandered in and out. Downstairs we had Christmas music, a buffet supper, and punch and cookies for the kids. Art Buchwald appeared midway through in a Santa Claus suit and passed out Christmas presents for everyone. Except for the children fighting over who got the best presents, the party was a huge success. And best of all, our friends had a guilt-free evening knowing they had actually done something with their kids instead of just going out to another boozy Christmas party.

Art and his late wife, Ann, used to have a legendary Easter egg hunt where he dressed up as the Easter Bunny and gave out prizes for the most eggs found. He stopped it when his kids got too old. But then, because he was Quinn's godfather, he and Ann decided to start it up again when Quinn and their grandchildren started coming along. It was a major production, and I think they did it once that time around and called it a day. But it was fun. We all love watching our friends' children grow up.

If you're going to have your kids appear at your grown-up parties, for God's sake don't make them perform. Unless your daughter is playing Annie on Broadway, I don't want to see these poor children forced to humiliate themselves in front of their parents' friends.

My father still has a searing memory of being made to play the guitar in front of his father's friends when he really wasn't very good, and just wanting to disappear through the floor.

My sister and I will never forgive my parents for the time—and it was the only time—they made us sing at one of their dinner parties. Donna and I had learned the words to "The Tennessee Waltz," and we liked to belt it out in a honky-tonk accent in the car. My parents thought we were adorable and funny and wanted us to sing it to their guests. We were not adorable. We were budding teenagers, pudgy and spotty, and though Donna had quite a nice voice, I couldn't carry a tune in a paper bag. (I was later exempted from mandatory glee club in high school.) I'll never forget the frozen smiles as Donna and I put on our painful little performance. We have never let my parents forget that atrocity, and they are still apologizing even though it has become a favorite family legend.

Still, I can't get that image out of my mind every time I see some poor kid dragged from his or her bedroom to show off for the parents' friends.

When Quinn was about seven or eight he had a bad habit of creeping downstairs after his bedtime when we were having seated dinners and harassing me.

"Mom, may I stay up late and watch a movie?"—on a school night. "Mom, may I have some extra candy?" "Mom, will you buy me a Swiss army knife?"

He knew perfectly well that I would say yes to anything to have him go to bed and not keep interrupting the conversation.

Finally I'd had enough. I told him in no uncertain terms that when we were having a dinner party I wanted him to go to bed and stay in bed and not keep coming down and trying to blackmail me.

"Unless the house is burning down, I don't want to see you after I've put you to bed on the night of a dinner party," I said sternly.

Sure enough, the very next party we had, down comes Quinn in his pajamas and stands over in the corner hissing at me.

"Mom! Mom!" he kept saying.

Annoyed, I kept whispering at him to go back to bed. He

refused and kept hissing at me. Finally, totally exasperated, I got up from my seat and went over to him.

"All I can say is that the house better be on fire or you're in real trouble, buster," I said to him.

"Mom," he said, "I've been trying to tell you. The President is on the phone!"

Apparently the President was trying to reach one of our guests and was indeed on the line.

Boy, did I eat crow. He's still making me pay for that one.

Forget pets. Pets do not make the cut, not even for cocktails. Lock them up, get them out of the way, send them to the vet's, loan them to a friend.

No, I am not antianimal. I am devoted to our four-year-old shih tzu, Sparky Crowninshield Bradlee, but Sparky is not ready for prime time. Neither are most pets. One couple I know had a dog who bit half the guests who came into the house. This is not cute.

They also get in the way. When you're having a cocktail party, people can trip over them. I nearly broke my ankle tripping over somebody's dog once. They bark, they drool, they shed, they jump up on you and dirty your dress or rip your stockings.

I once went to a party and this huge dog went right up and began sniffing one of the women guests. The more she pulled away, the more he did it. She was obviously mortified.

"Oh, don't worry," said the hostess, inappropriately amused at her guest's discomfort. "He's just a North American crotch hound."

This was not acceptable.

One of the biggest problems with pets is that a lot of people are allergic to them, even dogs. My husband is one of those people. He's horribly allergic to cats. He can be in a room with a cat for five minutes and his eyes become swollen little slits and he starts sneezing and can't breathe. It's gotten to the point now where he either doesn't go if he knows there are cats, or we call ahead and ask people to put their cats away, or he takes antihistamines, which don't really work.

One Washington hostess, Joan Braden, who used to have very swell parties, also had eight kids. (Her husband, columnist Tom Braden, wrote a book called *Eight Is Enough*, which was made into a TV sitcom.) Many of the children collected interesting, shall we say, pets. One of them was a boa constrictor. Alice Roosevelt Longworth, then in her nineties, used to love the boa and insist on wrapping it around herself when she went there. I did not. I am not amused at the idea of having a boa constrictor slithering around under the table when I'm trying to eat my filet mignon and discuss whether NATO should be expanded.

The point is, think of your guests' comfort first when you're deciding what to do with your pets.

Journalists Eleanor Randolph and Peter Pringle have great parties, mostly for other rowdy journalists, and they always have terrific food. One night they had a big bash and a groaning table with food they had been cooking for two days. After the party was over, Eleanor went into the dining room and was horrified to see that hardly anything had been eaten. When a friend called the next day she asked what had happened. Well, said the friend, it all looked lovely, but unfortunately Waldo the cat had stationed himself in the center of the table and, after helping himself, hissed menacingly at anyone who dared to get near the food. The guests were all too scared to eat, for fear of being mauled.

Finally, speaking of guests being mauled, there is the question of whether you should ever have reporters covering your parties. At your peril, is my feeling. At your peril.

We talked earlier about "safe" houses, meaning that you knew you would not get a really terrible seat at dinner. There is another kind of safe house too, and that is where you can feel secure you won't be pounced upon by a reporter covering the party.

Reporters are not really part of the entertainment. Part of the entertainment should not be seeing your guests and/or the host or hostess skewered in the next day's paper or a magazine.

I am speaking from experience. I was a party reporter. The whole idea is to hide behind a palm tree and listen to the guests saying stupid things, which you then write down and put in the paper. This is not always the case, and there are certainly decent, benign reporters and columnists out there who are not interested in personally destroying your reputation. But the same advice goes for them as it does for your guests. Know your reporters before you invite them in. I almost never do it, but every once in a while I will invite a reporter to cover a book party for a friend in hopes of getting some good publicity for the book.

You may love the idea of a delightful write-up of your tea for your favorite charity or the luncheon you give for the visiting celebrity, who is in town to perform. But it won't be so delightful if the piece turns out to be a hatchet job and embarrasses both you and your guests.

If you care about your guests, just know that inviting a reporter could not only cause them discomfort but also put them in jeopardy. And it would mean that . . . yours is not a safe house.

I generally pride myself on having a safe house in both senses of the word, even though at my parties there are usually more reporters than anybody else. But there is a thing called a "too good" story. This means that even though something is off the record or you know you're not supposed to write it or tell it, it's just too good not to. There's really not a whole lot a host or hostess can do about this one either.

It's happened to me twice—both times, I'm sorry to say, with Colin Powell and both times on New Year's Eve. The first time was at the start of 1991, the year that would bring the Gulf War, but by New Year's there was still no announcement or acknowledgment from the President about whether or not the United States would go to war against Saddam Hussein.

Colin Powell was chairman of the joint chiefs, and the minute he walked into the room he was surrounded by reporters questioning him about the government's plans. He was the Sphinx throughout most of the evening. But finally, toward midnight, *Post* columnist Richard Cohen walked up to him and asked if he personally should plan on going on a reporting trip to Iraq.

"Not," said Powell solemnly, "unless you want to come home in a body bag."

You can't imagine how the word spread through the party, and the next few days, without quoting Powell, there was a rash of stories about how inside sources were saying that the United States was preparing for war.

This past New Year's Eve, Colin Powell was again a guest. As midnight loomed, he was standing near the dance floor, as usual, surrounded by a group of reporters. Larry King was talking to another group when the DJ started to play "Auld Lang Syne."

Did Larry King grab his date and kiss her?

No way. With Al and Tipper Gore, Betty Bacall, and Tom and Meredith Brokaw only a few feet away, Larry grabbed Colin Powell, kissed him on the cheek, and began waltzing him around the dance floor. Powell, without missing a beat, turned to the gang of journalists agape on the sidelines and said with a beatific smile, "Don't ask, don't tell."

This is what is called a "too good" story.

It ended up—guess where?—in the *Washington Post* the next day.

Ben and I were not the source, Colin.

CHAPTER 11

The
Guest

"Look out, everyone, Sally's in labor."

Just because you're a guest does not mean that you are off the hook. A guest has obligations too.

The first obligation is to respond. You would be surprised how many people simply don't bother to answer an invitation. Some people gamely insert self-addressed stamped envelopes with a little card for you to check off whether or not you're coming. I don't do that. Half the people throw them away, and then you've spent all that money for nothing. Some optimists give a date by which time you should reply. I don't do that either. Nobody pays attention. What I do is call, or have somebody call, several days before the event. In Washington most people don't know what they're going to be doing three or four weeks in advance, because for so many politicians and journalists, life is dependent on breaking news and the events of the day. But a lot of people use that as an excuse. I'm-too-busy-and-important-to-reply-to-an-invitation kind of thing.

I have to admit that I am sometimes lax about answering invitations for receptions or book parties, but it really isn't right, because the host or hostess has to plan on the food, and if they've invited a lot of people, the money can really add up.

We also have the problem, like many busy couples, of trying to work out a system to control invitations. Sometimes they come to Ben's office and sometimes they come to the house. We have a system where the office invitations get faxed to the house and I also get copies from Ben's secretary, Carol, and I try to go over all of the invitations that come to the house with her every week. But I'm sorry to say that things still occasionally fall through the cracks and I know that happens to everyone sometimes.

We have a special problem though. Ben's briefcase. I call it the Bermuda Triangle. It's amazing how things get put in there and simply disappear forever.

If I'm having a P.R.F. (over a hundred people) I don't even try to call people I haven't heard from. I count on about a thirty to forty percent dropout of those asked and about one third to one fourth of the guests don't even bother to R.S.V.P. I'm pretty stoic by now, but this can really upset people who try to plan. The only problem with not calling is that sometimes people just don't get the invitation and never even know they've been asked and there can be badly hurt feelings.

I have to say, if there is someone who never bothers to R.S.V.P., I just stop inviting him or her. I also have to say that if you start entertaining, you automatically become a better guest. It's very enlightening to see it from another side.

Aside from the R.S.V.P., the guest has a number of other obligations. You should try to show up by fifteen minutes after the designated time (this is called fashionably late) but certainly no later than half an hour. If the hostess has a forty-five-minute cocktail period, that should allow you enough time to have a drink. I don't expect anyone to be there on the dot, and I don't like to arrive exactly then either, but it isn't fair to come waltzing in an hour later just as everyone is sitting down to dinner unless you have informed the hostess beforehand.

I think a guest owes it to the host or hostess to make an effort. You certainly wouldn't know this sometimes to see people standing in the corner not talking to anyone. I know it's awkward if you don't know anyone, but my feeling is, if you don't and can't talk to people, then you probably ought to stay for one drink and then leave. Obviously you can't do this if you're at a seated dinner, a wedding, or some sort of obligatory event, but I know if I'm not participating I am out of there. It's a downer for the other guests, who feel guilty if they see somone lurking in the corner and they don't feel like breaking away from their friends to talk to a stranger.

Guests should get around, mix and mingle, try to talk to everyone, be lively, and make an effort to look like they are having a good time. A guest should bring energy into a room, not suck the oxygen out of it.

You should dress properly. You shouldn't get drunk. You shouldn't be rude to any of the other guests, you shouldn't be ill mannered, and if you're a man you shouldn't make physical passes at the women. If you're a woman, however, it's OK.

Years ago, when I was seventeen, I went with my parents to a cocktail party given by Gwen Cafritz. It was the classic Washington summer-evening reception, held on her spacious lawn, filled with congressmen, senators, ambassadors, members of the cabinet, and White House officials. After mingling for a while, my mother —an extremely attractive and sexy woman—and I headed over to the buffet table to get something to eat. As we were reaching for the shrimp, both of us jumped and let out a little shriek simultaneously. As we looked around to see what had happened, there was Sen. Strom Thurmond, grinning from ear to ear, one hand on my behind and one on my mother's, there for all the world to see.

As I recall we were both quite flattered at the time and thought it was terribly funny and wicked of ole Strom.

Needless to say, this would not fly in the nineties.

Years later, during Watergate, and at the beginning of the feminist movement, when I was a reporter at the *Post*, I was on a panel at a journalism convention. The subject was the problems and circumstances women journalists face. I made a comment that if a senator had his hand on my fanny and was about to tell me whether he would vote to impeach Nixon, I wasn't sure I wouldn't wait until after he'd told me before I removed his hand. I was nearly booed off the stage and roundly excoriated by my colleagues, both verbally and in print.

I never said so at the time, but what made me think of that hypothetical in the first place was that affectionate little pat of Strom's when I was very young.

(By the way, if I had to make that speech today I'd definitely say I'd wait until after he gave me the story before removing his hand. Ha! That'll get them going again.)

So, guys, the old days of feeling up the woman sitting next to you under the table are over. Besides being sexist and gross, it is also politically incorrect. And it could be dangerous. You could get a smack in the puss, as my mother would say. I mention this because men feeling up women at parties still happens a lot. I'm not kidding.

However, a woman feeling up men at a party is a different story. At one of our New Year's Eve parties a few years ago, a good friend of mine who is a total babe had a few too many and took out after several of the men, giving them the real treatment. The guys were extremely flattered, if not somewhat astonished. Everyone was talking about it, the level of sexual energy went off the charts (this is Washington, after all), and it made the party.

I know. Life is not fair.

A guest should not smoke in someone's private home unless he asks the host or hostess first, or unless others are smoking.

Frankly, though, I don't think he ought to put his hosts in that position, because even if they don't mind, you can be sure some of the guests will. In fact, today, the majority of the guests will. This is a very American thing. Foreigners think we're crazy.

My feeling is that if you really have to smoke you should just quietly step outside and not force the issue. If I'm a hostess and I'm asked, I will say OK. It doesn't bother me, but I worry that it might offend a number of the other guests. Since my role is to consider everyone, I would rather there be no smoking. However,

I would never ask a guest who lights up not to smoke unless another guest complains about it. And I always have plenty of ashtrays around, just in case.

A guest should never bring another friend to a party without asking, and you really shouldn't ask to bring somebody to a very personal party like an anniversary party or wedding unless you are living together or dating seriously. To ask to bring a date to something important just to have a date is pushing it, and it puts the host or hostess in a terrible position. The incredible thing is how often people show up with friends or dates to seated parties without calling first. This happens more often in Washington, where senators and congressmen travel with entourages and will often arrive at a cocktail party with two or three in tow. I've never had it happen at a seated dinner myself, but I've seen it and it is—how shall I say this?—ugly.

It's really not up to a guest to criticize the host or hostess unless there is a legitimate reason to make a suggestion, like, "It appears to be sleeting; do you think we could go inside and finish our hamburgers?" or something like that. It's really not acceptable to criticize the food. If you don't like it, don't eat it, and if it's really bad, just don't accept any more invitations from that person.

Many years ago I was at a small dinner given by a Washington hostess who was particularly pleased to snag columnist Joe Alsop as her guest. All went well at the dinner table until the main course was served. The hostess's personal chef had prepared leeks, and they were quite delicious, though a bit difficult to cut. With the entire table listening, Joe turned to the hostess and said in a loud voice, "My dear, these are impossible to eat. You must tell your chef—one always quarters the leeks."

She was horribly embarrassed, and so were the other guests. It humiliated her and made everyone feel bad, including the poor chef, who I'm sure heard about it that night.

I've never served leeks since without quartering them, though.

When should a guest help the hostess serve or clear the table? I can't stand this thing of everyone jumping up to help the hostess, leaving a half-empty table. It really ruins a party. If I'm the hostess at a small informal dinner and have no help, I generally try to do it myself so that the conversation can continue uninterrupted. If I need help I'll usually ask one person to help me. Generally someone will offer, and if I want their help I'll say so. If I don't, I will insist they stay put. As a guest I'm happy to help and will try to offer, but I'm often not as fast as the jumper-uppers, most of whom are usually women. If everyone else gets up I will stay at the table on the theory that somebody needs to stay behind and keep things going.

I was at a party recently where so many people got up to help that we all ended up in the kitchen. It upset the hostess but she still didn't take charge. It pretty much squelched the conversation, and everyone had coffee and went home. I'd rather do it myself and have the guests have a great time without their feeling guilty that they didn't leap up and clear the table.

One of the most annoying things a guest can do is change place cards if they don't like where they are sitting. Presumably the host or hostess has gone to a lot of thought and trouble to try to put people where they think they will have the best time. And they know a lot about the guests that you may not know. It is really inexcusable to take it upon yourself to make a change just because you want a more prestigious seat. If you simply don't like your seat, just live with it, and don't go back if you have a terrible time. If it's really a disaster, like you're not speaking to the person, talk to the hostess, explain the situation, and ask her to please change the seat. I have actually mentioned to my hostess on one occasion that I had been seated next to "Horace" three times in the last few weeks and I thought he might be bored sitting next to me again. Usually the hostess is grateful for that kind of information and will agree to change the seating if it's not too hectic.

I once had a dinner party for twelve at a long table. When I finally made my way to the dining room I found, to my dismay, that one of my guests had changed the seating, which she admitted to, because she thought she would have more fun with another man. Unbeknownst to her, however, she had placed the woman with whom she had traded seats next to a man who had just destroyed her best friend in print and to whom she was not speaking. It was too late for me to do anything about it without embarrassing everyone, but it really ruined the dinner.

Should the guest bring something or send something to the party? I do not think it is necessary, and I almost never do. If you want to send flowers beforehand, particularly if it's a party in your honor, you can do that. But send something simple and elegant like a large bouquet of white roses or white lilies or pale peonies. If you know what your hostess's house looks like and what her taste is, you can be more imaginative. But if you don't, then make sure you send something that will go with any decor or color scheme. I'm of two minds about this. I think it's a wonderful gesture, but if I'm having a party I most likely have already bought or ordered the flowers, and often I'm faced with a bouquet that doesn't fit. I don't want to offend the sender, and yet I don't want to put out something that I don't like. Make sure, if you're sending flowers the day of the party, that they arrive in a vase so the hostess doesn't have to scurry around trying to find one at the last minute.

Under no circumstances should you show up at the door with flowers unless it is a small informal party and you are sure it won't be disruptive. It's a hassle for the hostess to try to find a vase and arrange flowers while greeting her guests and getting her party started.

I also don't advise sending flowers the next day. The flowers the hostess already has for the party will last at least four or five days, so why not wait and send flowers in a week, when the others will have died and they will be so much more appreciated?

I went to a party in Hollywood, at a private house, that was lavish, with a band, tent, and the most beautiful flowers you've ever seen. We were staying at the host's house, and the next day dozens of $300–$400 bouquets began arriving from guests with thank you notes. I've never seen anything like it. And all I could think was, what a waste. There was no place to put them because the house was already filled with flowers from the night before.

Speaking of bringing flowers, when I lived in Germany years ago I had a German beau who was gorgeous, romantic, and poetic, but short on cash. I was just out of college, living with my parents, and working at Daimler Benz. My father was the commanding general of the Seventh Army at the time, and we lived in a mansion on a large estate in Stuttgart. Each time I had a date with this man, he never failed to arrive with the most beautiful flowers. I couldn't understand how he could afford them until one day, when we had been going out for several months, he confessed that he was picking them from our garden on his way in.

I don't advise this.

What about bringing wine to a party? This is a nice gesture, one that I appreciate. Just don't expect the hostess to use it if she has already chosen the wine for the evening. Depending on the size of the party and who's there, I often will open a bottle brought by a guest. If it doesn't fit with my menu I'll thank the guest and put it away for another time.

Hostess gifts are nice, but I have to say that when the guests are arriving you don't have time to acknowledge the gifts, and half the time you don't even know people have brought things until the next morning. I always end up worrying that I've missed a present that was left. I've had people leave things with no notes, so I can't thank them, and I've found gifts months later that had fallen behind a table or sofa. If it's a big party I would suggest sending something later just so you'll get brownie points and the hostess won't suffer terminal guilt not knowing who brought her what. I don't ever bring hostess gifts, for that reason, but it doesn't mean that I haven't gotten some lovely things that pleased me enormously. Actually, to me, the perfect hostess gift is to have the guest arrive with a smile, make an effort, and have a great time.

If you break or spill something you should certainly send a gift or flowers. If it requires a minor repair or cleaning and you can afford it, you should offer to pay. If it's a priceless Ming vase you obviously can't afford to replace it unless you're Bill Gates, but you need to apologize profusely. Just know that any host or hostess has got to be prepared for that sort of thing. It goes with the territory. No matter how serious the damage, unless the guest has caused it deliberately, if it's your house you have no choice but to be gracious. If you have really priceless things you ought to put them away for P.R.F.'s. If you can't handle the basic wear and tear of having a party, then you just shouldn't entertain at home.

One of the most famous ambassadors who ever came to Washington was an Iranian named Ardeshir Zahedi. He had been posted here twice, once in the early sixties, when he was married to Princess Shanaz, the shah's daughter, and later in the seventies, after he was divorced. The first time around he had been very close to my parents, and though I was away at college, I got to know him quite well.

I will never forget the night he showed up at our quarters at Fort Myer, the army post where we were living, next to Arlington

National Cemetery. My parents were having a cocktail party and Ardeshir walked in the door carrying a huge Santa Claus–sized bag. Without saying a word he turned the bag over and emptied it onto the floor. Out poured thousands of Iranian pistachio nuts, which he knew my mother adored. Instead of disrupting the party it only added to the fun. Everyone ended up sitting on the floor drinking and shelling and eating nuts and laughing and telling stories until all hours of the night.

The second time around as ambassador, Ardeshir was divorced and was extremely sought after as a bachelor. He was good looking, rich, and powerful, plus he was a lot of fun and loved to entertain. He also had some of the best parties in town. Ardeshir was well known for being extravagant, and one of the things he did was send tins of Iranian caviar instead of thank you notes to those who had had him for dinner.

One day I was shopping with Barbara Howar when she called home for messages. She had had a dinner the night before at which Ardeshir had been a guest, so when her housekeeper told her that a package had been hand delivered from the Iranian embassy we both knew for certain that it was caviar.

Without missing a beat she asked her housekeeper to make some toast, chop some onion, boil some eggs, and chop them up with the whites separate, and announced that we would be home in half an hour. We raced back to her house where the toast, onion, and eggs were all neatly chopped up on a plate with an iced caviar dish next to them and a small spoon. Barbara quickly tore the wrapping paper off the gift and found a small box inside. Puzzled, she opened the box to find, to our dismay, a porcelain cigarette box with a photograph of the shah and his family superimposed on it. Apparently, people all over town were getting the same present, and within days the word was out. The shah was about to be overthrown. And it was true. So you see how the "most frivolous" things can portend "the sternest purpose," as Arthur Schlesinger noted.

Which brings us to thank you notes.

Do you have to write a thank you note after every party?

I am the worst person to ask because I have a mental block about writing thank you notes. It's almost pathological. The only excuse I can think of is that because I'm a writer I feel I can't just dash off a note saying, "Thank you so much for the lovely party. Ben and I had a wonderful time . . ." I think that I'm expected to write something witty and clever, and the idea of it just stops me cold, so I don't write anything. This doesn't mean that I don't suffer terrible guilt about not writing, though.

When my first novel was published (or was it my book on my disastrous television experience at CBS News, where I bombed as the first female network anchor in America? I can't remember), I made a speech in Dallas, Texas, while on my promotion tour. An old college chum, Peggy Seay Oglesby, lived in Dallas and she had a wonderful party for me. I never wrote her a thank you note and I still feel guilty about it. I lost her address, or some such excuse, it doesn't matter. Anyway, I'm sorry, Peggy, and thanks for a great party.

For normal events I don't think a note is ever necessary. For major events it is nice but still not obligatory. Though I'm always pleased to receive them, I certainly don't expect thank you notes. After all, if you have done your part to make the party a success, then that's thanks enough for me.

I have one celebrity friend who hates to write notes and joked to me recently that she didn't write them because "they're lucky to have me." She was right. She is a great guest, if not the most modest.

It's never a good idea, if you're a pregnant guest, to show up at a party in labor. I'm not sure I would call this a matter of etiquette, but there's nothing like a woman having closely timed contractions to kill an evening.

I actually did this, and it was a disaster.

It happened this way. I was three weeks past my due date when I began having contractions late one afternoon at the hairdresser's. When I got home I called the doctor, who insisted that I was not ready to come in yet and told me to phone him around midnight. We had accepted a dinner invitation at Johnny and Teresa Heinz's. Johnny, who died a few years later, was the senator from Pennsylvania, and Teresa is now married to Sen. John Kerry of Massachusetts. Ben thought it would be crazy to go, but I insisted. I needed to be distracted, and besides, my contractions were still fairly far apart and they weren't terribly painful yet. Ben finally relented but made me promise to tell him the minute I thought I might be in trouble.

As we pulled up to the Heinzes' we both agreed that we would not tell anyone I was in labor. We would just pretend everything was fine, and nobody would ever know.

You can imagine my shock when we walked into the living room filled with people and Ben announced in his loudest voice, "Look out, everyone, Sally's in labor!"

In retrospect, the look of horror that came over the assembled faces was hilarious as they all unconsciously took several steps backward to distance themselves from me. I will be forever grateful to my host, Johnny Heinz, who walked toward me with his arms wide open, a big grin on his face, and embraced me as if I were his long-lost friend. Talk about the perfect host!

We went in to dinner shortly, and I was seated between columnist Joseph Kraft, who had never had children, and the senator from Washington State, Scoop Jackson, both of whom have since died. I have never seen two more desperate men in my entire life. They tried valiantly to carry on a conversation around me because I was completely incapable of putting two words to-gether. Never mind that they were talking about Boeing, located in the senator's state, about which I knew nothing and cared even less. Instead of the party being a distraction to me, the contractions were a distraction from the party. Every four minutes or so I would grimace, shut my eyes, and give a short little grunt. Both of them would stop talking, their eyes on sticks, their lips dry, their fore-heads perspiring, and search frantically around the room as if for an emergency exit. They looked as if they had visions in their heads of having to boil water and sever the umbilical cord with their teeth.

Mercifully for all of us the dinner ended, and to the undis-guised relief of the other guests, not to mention my dinner part-ners, Ben and I beat a hasty retreat.

Quinn wasn't born until twenty-seven hours later. But who knew?

Never cancel to accept a better offer.

This is one of the toughest rules for a guest ever and one that I have broken only rarely, and then I didn't feel good about it.

And please don't compound the error by accepting a better offer and lying about it to your original host or hostess. It almost never works. People inevitably find out about it, they get hurt feelings, you get a bad reputation if you do it often enough, and if you have any conscience at all, you end up feeling awful yourself. It just isn't worth it.

In Washington, however, there is one exception. That is an invitation to the White House or to have dinner with the Presi-dent. This is simply understood.

A perfect example of this took place the year Bill Clinton got elected President. In November, a few weeks after the election, David and Susan Brinkley sent out beautiful engraved invitations to a Christmas cocktail buffet in December. There was no guest of honor; it was just a gathering of friends. We were invited and accepted with pleasure. The Brinkleys always have wonderful parties. It was the first Christmas party of the season, and we were happy to be going.

Unfortunately, Katharine Graham had planned to have a dinner for the Clintons, and the evening of the Brinkleys' party was the only night they could do it. It's safe to say that at least half of Kay's guest list turned out to be on the Brinkleys'. All over Washington, people who had accepted the Brinkleys' invitation were getting Kay's and feeling sick. Hardly any of those on either guest list, mostly those in the Washington establishment, knew the Clintons well. Many of them were hoping for jobs in the administration, and a lot of them were journalists who were writing about and would continue to write about the President. Seeing him at his first small, intimate, private gathering would be very valuable professionally, not to mention socially, for the majority of guests. On the other hand, everyone loves David and Susan and certainly did not want to hurt or offend them.

The phone lines were working overtime that week. People were desperate. Nobody knew what to do.

I can barely write this, I am so ashamed, but I was one of those who decided to go to Kay's. I called Susan, one of the most difficult phone calls I have ever made. All I can say is that Susan, who is totally savvy about Washington, responded with class and grace. She was completely understanding and tried to make me feel better about backing out of her party.

We went to Kay's, and professionally it was a very valuable evening for me. I got three pieces for the paper and one column for *Newsweek* out of background information I picked up and observations that I made from that one evening, not to mention stories for this book and scenes for a novel I'm working on. This doesn't count the intangible vibes and atmospherics I absorbed that evening and was able to talk about in television interviews.

Still, I never felt great about it. I don't know what I would have done if I had been Susan. I might have just been as cynical as some of my guests and simply changed the date of my party.

The only thing I can think of that would make it worthwhile to accept a better offer is to be able to use the line one of my friends did when he called the hostess of the first invitation and told her that he had accepted "a subsequent invitation."

So, is the guest always right? Is it true, as my father said so memorably, that a guest "can do no wrong"?

Well, not always.

Some years ago I had a farewell party for a departing British journalist. It was a buffet supper, and after much drinking and merrymaking the toasts began. All of a sudden, to my horror, one of the male guests jumped up on my beautiful white damask sofa with his shoes on and started emoting about the guest of honor. Before I could control myself I found that I was shouting from the opposite end of the room, "Get your goddamned shoes off my white sofa."

CHAPTER 12

The Point (Again)

I go into my total Zen mode and begin chanting my mantra:
"It's only a party, it's only a party, it's only a party."

The former speaker of the House and soon-to-be ambassador to Japan Tom Foley told me that he once was in a focus group of voters and a blue-collar worker had told him what his fantasy of the life of a congressman was like in Washington. The man told him that he just assumed that all congressmen rode around in huge stretch limousines being driven to fancy Washington dinner parties in Georgetown mansions only to be embarrassed that they didn't know what food to eat and which fork to eat it with.

It's not quite that way. But it is true that many newcomers to Washington, whether they are members of Congress or administration types or diplomats or journalists, do find the whole notion of Washington and Georgetown dinner parties terribly intimidating.

I hope that I have managed to put some of those fears to rest in this book by demystifying a lot of what goes on here.

For my sins, after I finished the first draft, I started having a terrible recurring party nightmare. The party nightmare was essentially the classic exam nightmare, only in a different setting. The exam nightmare, for those who have never had one, has you going to take the exam, only to realize that you haven't been to a single class or done any of the reading for the whole year.

My party nightmare goes like this: I'm having a huge, catered, seated dinner. The caterer arrives with the tables, only they're all different sizes and shapes and they don't fit in my dining room. The cloths are unbelievably ugly; none of them match and they don't fit the tables. The flower arrangements arrive and they are four-foot-tall bird-of-paradise arrangements. The food is not edible, and the caterers forgot the wine. But the worst is that I start to do the seating arrangement and realize that I can't remember who is coming to the party and I can't find a copy of the guest list. I wake up in a panic.

This is when I go into my total Zen mode and begin chanting my mantra, which should also be the mantra of any host or hostess with a brain in his or her head. "It's only a party, it's only a party, it's only a party." It is *not* the end of the world if things go wrong. In fact, it could be a book!

The fact is that everyone feels insecure and uncomfortable sometimes. That's why, no matter whether you are the host or the guest, it is important to focus on the reason you are doing all this in the first place.

The only things that matter are these: that people have a good time and that you remember the Golden Rule. Treat everyone the way you would like to be treated. Remember too that the party will never work if you are a nervous wreck, the guests are boring and awful, the food is disgusting, the wine doesn't flow, the evening is forced, formal, and stilted, and the guests don't feel wanted, celebrated, special, and cherished. Parties are about people, not about things.

Am I the perfect hostess? Of course not. Do I break my own rules? Absolutely. Do I make mistakes? All the time. I had to laugh when Eleanor Randolph called after having read the manuscript of this book and said she just knew that it was about her and all the mistakes she had made at her parties. But it's not about Eleanor at all. It's about me, it's about all of us. I can't even think of a party I've ever given where I haven't made at least one mistake. And sometimes they're big mistakes. And I'm sure I'll keep on making them for the rest of my life. I just hope I learn from them.

One of the worst was several years ago at a New Year's Eve party. An elderly couple showed up and I had no idea who they were, and neither did Ben. They introduced themselves and seemed quite happy to be there, and we came to the conclusion that they had simply crashed the party. We took several of our friends aside and asked them to find out something about the couple, but nothing rang a bell. We didn't dare confront them, but I was so annoyed that I virtually ignored them all night, even though they were guests in my house.

Later it turned out that their name had inadvertently been transposed by the computer in my husband's office onto the official guest list from some advertisers' list and they actually had been invited. I still haven't gotten over how rude I was to ignore them and how bad I felt for not being a more gracious hostess.

There is no such thing as perfection. You can only hope to have fun and make sure your guests do too. And remember, if the hostess isn't having fun, nobody else will either.

My father will be ninety on the first of November, and my mother will be eighty in January. My father was deathly ill last fall. He lost forty pounds, was hospitalized for several months, had surgery twice for cancer, and was not expected to live. His recuperation has been slow and painful. My mother, whose stroke has left her right arm totally paralyzed, has only partial use of her left arm and hand. She cannot walk without help, has had some loss of executive function, and has difficulty initiating plans. She requires a full-time nurse around the clock.

Have they slowed down? No way. It's party time at the Quinns' every Saturday night.

My parents have a country house on the Eastern Shore of Maryland, where they go on the weekends. They used to have an incredible social life there, with sometimes two and three parties to attend in a night, and they themselves were constantly entertaining.

Obviously, because my mother can no longer cook, they can't do it the way they used to, so my father has started having what he calls "Bette Quinn seminars." He invites two or three couples for cocktails. My mother has her nurse take her to town where she picks up some frozen pizza, microwave popcorn, and her favorite horseradish cheese and crackers. My father sets up the bar. When the guests arrive, my father asks the other men to make drinks for themselves and their wives. Everyone sits around the coffee table in the sunroom because my mother can't stand. They generally have some sort of discussion, sexual harassment in the military or something equally controversial that will get things going. And they all have a great time for close to two hours. The Bette Quinn seminars have become very popular outings on the Eastern Shore, with people clamoring for invitations.

How do they do it?

"I love people, darlin'," says my mother. "I love to entertain, and I always have fun."

"Bette and I plan to have a good time at our parties," says my father. "We're not constantly biting our fingernails and worrying about whether our guests will. We know they will because we will. We're optimists. We try to be friendly, genial, and hospitable, and it's contagious."

My father describes himself and my mother as "bon vivants." And that they are and always will be.

Isn't that what it's all about anyway? Living well? And where best to start than at "the party."